ACCIDENTS IN NORTH AMERICAN MOUNTAINEERING

VOLUME 8 • NUMBER 3 • ISSUE 56

2003

THE AMERICAN ALPINE CLUB
GOLDEN

THE ALPINE CLUB OF CANADA
BANFF

ISSN   0065-082X

ISBN   0-930410-94-7

Manufactured in the United States

Published by
The American Alpine Club, Inc.
710 Tenth Street, Suite 100
Golden, CO 80401

Cover Illustrations
Front: Descending Disappointment Cleaver on Mount Rainier. Photograph by Bob Potts.

Back: Parks Canada Warden Service, helicopter sling rescue, Mount Louis, Banff National Park. Photograph by Brad White, Parks Canada.

♻ Printed on recycled paper

CONTENTS

SAFETY COMMITTEES 2002

The American Alpine Club

Aram Attarian, John Dill, Mike Gauthier, Renny Jackson,
Daryl Miller, Jeff Sheetz, and John E. (Jed) Williamson *(Chair)*

The Alpine Club of Canada

Helmut Microys, Peter Amann, Peter Roginski,
Simon Ruel, Murray Toft *(Chair)*

ACCIDENTS IN
NORTH AMERICAN MOUNTAINEERING
Fifty-Sixth Annual Report of the Safety Committees
of The American Alpine Club and The Alpine Club of Canada

This is the fifty-sixth issue of *Accidents in North American Mountaineering* and the twenty-fifth issue in which The Alpine Club of Canada has contributed data and narratives.

Canada: Once again it was the year of the stranded climber in Canada, with five reported incidents where the parties involved got themselves into situations where they were unable to ascend or descend without assistance. Also of note were incidents of rockfall or icefall. Rapid changes in temperature increase the hazards and in the case of ice climbing, a rapid drop in temperatures leads to fracturing and can result in a catastrophic failure of ice formations. The fatality at Louise Falls was just such an incident. We are seeing an increased number of ice climbing accidents which correlates with an increase in the popularity of this sport. Lower extremity injuries are a common consequence of falling even a short distance while wearing crampons.

There are many accidents in Canada which are going unreported in this book. Once again, for reasons of lack of funding, it was not possible to provide comprehensive data from B.C. Parks. It is also difficult to obtain data for accidents outside of the Canadian Rockies region despite our attempts to solicit information. We are sure that there must be more accidents east of Alberta! If anyone has knowledge of a climbing accident, you are encouraged to report it to the Editor in the hopes of preventing similar accidents through sharing of information with others.

We wish to thank the following individuals for their contributions and assistance in tracking down information throughout the year: Nancy Hansen, Marc Ledwidge, Burke Duncan, Jim Mamalis, Brent Kozachenko, Ian Greant, Marcus Eyre, Dave Stephens, Paul Walton, Gord Irwin, Judy Lynne, Greg McDonnell, Mike Rogers, and Frederic Lebarre.

United States: Fatalities, at 34, were back to an above-average level for the past ten years. Given the variety and scope of climbing areas in the U.S. and given the numbers of climbers out there, it is hard to predict from year to year what the fatality and serious injury totals will be. The number of accidents reported each year seems to be holding steady. This is encouraging, because both the sport and the reporting network has grown.

Speaking of numbers, the Outdoor Industry Association has put forward an estimated count of persons 16 years or older who have "climbed at least once with a rope and harness on a natural rock surface" at six million. They put the number of "enthusiasts"—those who engage in this activity at least ten times per year—at 1.3 million. While they claim statistical reliability with the instrument they used, I find this number to defy what land managers, other climbers, and local knowledge tell me. I still stand by a number of 250-300,000. But the good news is that if the number IS 1.3 million, we are seeing a very low accident and fatality rate.

An interesting thing to ponder when considering consequences of a fall is: How far is too far to fall? The American College of Surgeons calls for assuming neck and back injuries, as well as fractures, for anyone who falls from a height greater than 20 feet. It seems that from the reports we receive, ten feet often leads to serious injury. This is why placing good protection at reasonable intervals is recommended. The trickiest part of any climb is when departing from the ground to the first piece of protection.

Inadequate protection and protection pulling out continue to figure heavily in direct and contributory causes for the injuries and fatalities, which is, of course, because falls in these cases are longer—including going all the way to the ground sometimes. Descending errors are mostly the result of lowering climbers rather than rappels. These are primarily due to ropes being too short (and no knot being tied in the end), speed build-up so the belayer can't hang on, and inadequate anchoring.

There were quite a few climbing areas that had no reports of accidents resulting in injuries or fatalities. Most noteworthy were Joshua Tree National Park and Devil's Lake State Park. Not seen in the narratives are three reports from City of Rocks—leader falls with not enough protection. The Climbing Ranger there, Brad Shilling, believes that 60-meter ropes have helped reduce belay/rappel accidents significantly, as has a focus on good communication skills. There was one incident from Montana. A falling rock set loose from climbers above on the East Ridge of Granite Peak resulted in a fractured hand to someone below—and his subsequent fall. Rangers from the Grand Tetons had to be called in for the rescue. Not ready in time for publication were four reports from Mount Orizaba in Mexico. We finally have a contact there!

In addition to the Safety Committee, we are grateful to the following— with apologies for any omissions—for collecting data and helping with the report: Hank Alicandri, Dave Brown, Jim Detterline, Erik Hansen Al Hospers, Chuck Lindsay, Mark Magnuson, Tom Moyer, Steve Muelhauser, Leo Paik, Steve Rollins, Brad Shilling, Robert Speik, Eric White, Willow Williamson, all individuals who sent in personal stories, and, of course, George Sainsbury.

John E. (Jed) Williamson
Managing Editor
7 River Ridge Road
Hanover, NH 03755
e-mail: jedwmsn@sover.net

Edwina Podemski
Canadian Editor
700 Phipps McKinnon Building
10020-101A Avenue
Edmonton, Alberta T5J 3G2
e-mail: cwep@compusmart.ab.ca

CANADA

FALL ON ICE, INADEQUATE PROTECTION
Alberta, Banff National Park, Bow Falls

On February 12, The Mountaineers party began their approach across the frozen lake at 9:00 a.m., with all on snowshoes except Gordon Schryer (32), who was on skis. They arrived at the base of the snow slope leading to Bow Falls about 11:00 a.m. A British party had geared up and were ascending to the base of the climb.

The British climbers chose a central line up Bow Falls. The Mountaineers party took their time getting ready to allow the British climbers time to get up the route. Schryer and his partner Chris Nowak (32) decided to climb a line to the left of the British team, while the other team decided to take the same line as the British team on a route rated III WI4. After Schryer and Nowak began climbing, a team of two climbers from Montana arrived and chose to climb a line to the right of center.

Schryer and Nowak began their climb, with Nowak leading first and Schryer belaying. Schryer wore a down jacket for warmth while he belayed. All were wearing helmets. The first pitch began in a gully with mixed snow and ice. Once he left the gully (which was difficult to protect) Nowak placed four ice screws for protection. He then set up a belay about 80 feet off the ground using three ice screws.

The ice quality was variable, reported as fairly solid in some places with air pockets and dinner-plating in others. Schryer followed the pitch with little difficulty. He was wearing crampons on his ski boots for the first time; he had worn plastic climbing boots on previous ice climbs.

At the belay, they consolidated gear. After this exchange, Schryer had six ice screws and a number of quick-draws. Schryer began leading the second pitch on a line that trended up and left from Nowak's belay. Schryer placed three ice screws about ten feet apart as he climbed. As he climbed he had trouble removing his tools from the ice. He reported that he was frustrated by this and attributed it to sinking the tools in deeper than usual to get a secure placement due to dinner-plating of the ice.

Just above the third ice screw Schryer followed an ice trough that angled up and right before it leveled off at two or three four-foot ice steps. The ice bulged somewhat above Schryer's third and last ice screw. At the first step, perhaps 30 feet above his last ice screw, Schryer met the British team, who were preparing a v-thread anchor for their rappel. (They had traversed a good distance from the top of their route.) They suggested that Schryer clip into their v-thread, but Schryer declined. Schryer climbed up to the next step. A Brit reported that the next time he noticed Schryer he was trying to catch his balance, taking small backward steps. Then Schryer fell down the slope and over the edge. He passed close enough to the British team to reach toward them, but he was out of reach.

Schryer fell past Nowak, who was able to hold the fall. Nowak was pulled into the ice by the force of the fall. The ice screws placed by Schryer all held. Nowak shouted to Schryer but got no response. He could, however, hear what sounded like snoring, which confirmed that Schryer was breathing. No one on the route could see Schryer at this time. However, all knew what happened and began communicating about how to respond.

Nowak lowered Schryer somewhat in an attempt to position him in the initial gully. A Brit rappelled down two 60-meter ropes and assessed Schryer's condition. He was initially unconscious, then regained consciousness. The Brit and Nowak coordinated lowering Schryer, with the Brit rappelling along side him for support.

Schryer was semi-conscious with bleeding cuts evident. He had vomited blood. Schryer reported pain in his right knee and shoulders when touched. The other Montana climber arrived. Nowak had him collect warm clothing from the packs just below and bring them up to help keep Schryer warm. They positioned an empty pack and coiled ropes under him to insulate him from the snow. Despite this effort Schryer shivered and complained of the cold. The other Mountaineer rope team arrived during this time. They had to complete the final pitch in order to descend safely. They cleaned Schryer's pitch upon descent and found that all three ice screws were secure.

Schryer was helicoptered to the lodge and taken by ambulance to Calgary where he was treated for a basal skull fracture and other injuries and released several days later.

Analysis

The immediate cause of the accident was a fall on ice, with inadequate protection as a contributing cause. Schryer himself remembers almost nothing of the accident, and can offer no explanation for either declining to clip the Brit's protection or not placing other protection on the last 30 feet. While Schryer had five years of experience in rock and alpine climbing, this was only his second season on water ice. Banff Warden Percy Woods commented that placing an ice screw before the transition from steep ice to less-steep ice at the top of a waterfall is important because climbers are more likely to fall as they change over from front-pointing technique to flat-footing. This transition can be awkward. He said that falls at the transition are the second most common cause of waterfall ice climbing injuries in the park—after getting hit by snow and ice falling from above. (Source: Steve Firebaugh, The Mountaineers)

FALLING ICICLE, FALL ON ICE, INADEQUATE PROTECTION
Alberta, Waterton Lakes National Park, Cameron Lake Road, Pearl Necklace
On March 2, a climber was five to seven meters into a lead on Pearl Necklace (50 m. WI 5+), without placing any protection. He had placed a tool

and kicked one foot into a free-hanging icicle when it broke. The climber barn-doored backward, then fell, hitting the ground shortly after the large icicle. He landed feet first then rolled a short distance downslope. He suffered a broken tibia and fibula in his left leg.

Analysis

The climber gambled on an unprotected move onto a risky icicle, with the potential of groundfall as a consequence. (Source: Parks Canada Warden Service, Brent Kozachenko)

FALLING ICE
Alberta, Banff National Park, Louise Falls II WI4+

On March 7, three climbers were climbing the left line of Louise Falls. The temperature in the Lake Louise area had been at around zero degrees C, then dropped to -26 degrees C in the couple of days before March 7. The lead climber had lead the left edge of the crux pillar and up to a tree belay. He led the route using two 60-meter 8.5mm ropes. His two partners were anchored to two ice screws below the left edge of the pillar. The lead climber brought up most of the slack in both ropes up to the top belay. He clipped the one rope into the end of his daisy chain and put the other line on belay. Climber #2 was belayed up to the anchor. J.D. (37) was waiting in the belay cave to begin his ascent of the final pitch. The rope to J.D. suddenly became taut with sufficient force to blow out all but the last bartacks in the lead climber's daisy chain. J.D. had been standing in a cave under a large veil of hanging ice. This veil of ice cracked off, fell and crushed him when the ropes dragged him into the path of the ice. He fell 10 to 15 meters down the face of the ice climb and came to rest hanging from his harness on the rope.

Two other climbers were just approaching the base of the pillar on the climber's right hand side when the accident occurred. They rappelled at an angle over to the fallen climber and reported that the victim had no vital signs—no pulse, pupils fixed and dilated. The two other climbers lowered the victim to the bottom of the climb. The accident was reported to Warden Service Dispatch and the deceased victim was later evacuated by helisling by Warden Service rescue crews.

Analysis

Free hanging icicles and veils of ice pose a hazard to climbers at any time. Hazards are increased whenever there is rapid and significant change in temperatures, as ice responds by contracting or expanding. This can cause the ice to crack and to become more susceptible to breaking. An earlier climbing party had noticed the ice near the pillar had made loud cracking noises twice during their ascent. They were unconcerned because the crux pillar was supported from below and their route was not underneath any free hanging curtains. It is unclear whether the victim's party was present when these cracking noises occurred. (Source: Parks Canada Warden Service, Marc Ledwidge, Edwina Podemski)

FALL ON ICE, PROTECTION PULLED OUT—ICE TOOL
Alberta, Banff National Park, Professor Falls,
On March 10 at 1130, T.M. was leading the last pitch of Professor Falls (III WI4). She was having some difficulty placing a screw due to the brittle nature of the ice and clipped the rope into her tool to rest. She was a little over ten meters above her last piece. When she weighted the rope to rest, her tool pulled. She fell 25 meters and broke her right ankle in the fall. Her partner, R.H., lowered her to the bottom of the pitch and improvised a splint for her leg. Because her pack with extra clothes, food, ensolite and thermos was down at the bottom of the next pitch, the party took some time to lower and rappel down to that point before R.H. left to get help. T.M. was later evacuated by heli-sling by Warden Service rescue crews. (Source: Parks Canada Warden Service, Marc Ledwidge)

FALL THROUGH CORNICE, OFF ROUTE, UNROPED
Alberta, Banff National Park, Mount Balfour
On April 12, N.F., a ski patroller from Whistler and member of the ACC Whistler section, was skiing the Wapta Icefield traverse with two companions, D.S. and G.M. They were equipped with a copy of Murray Toft's Wapta Traverse composite topo map and compasses. They had conversed with guides at one of the huts who had informed them that the snowpack was large this year. The visibility over the previous few days had been intermittent with some whiteout conditions. They had had no trouble with crevasses on the traverse. When they reached the Balfour Hut, they were joined by another party of two, S.F. and E.N., who were equipped with a GPS, compasses and an emergency radio. The two groups decided to combine forces on the ascent over the Balfour High Col to the Scott Duncan Hut.

They were skiing roped up in two teams. The skiers were using a Rutschblock cord tied to their ski poles and flicking it ahead of them to assist in defining the changes in the terrain. They periodically checked their bearings by compass and GPS and switched leaders. At one point N.F. believed that the group had veered too far left and corrected their course. As the group climbed toward the Col, visibility was initially quite reasonable and no worse than on previous days. As the group approached what they believed was the Col, the visibility dropped sharply. They were actually off-route to the extreme left edge of the traverse at this point.

The group checked their bearings by GPS and decided to unrope for the descent, as they felt they were beyond the obvious crevasses and could navigate reasonably well. They also removed their skins and Rutschblock cords and were having to travel shoulder to shoulder at that point in order to keep track of each other in the whiteout conditions. Each member was using a compass and/or GPS. N.F. was using a compass. His closest companion, G.M., noticed that he pushed off a couple times and then took a reading on his compass. He skied off away from the group, slightly to the left. It was at that moment, when N.F. was about 20 to 25 feet away, that

N.F. disappeared. N.F.'s companion was clearly also very close to the edge. G.M. believed that N.F. had skied over a wind lip. He skied toward N.F. but was warned by another member of the party to get back from the edge. It was then that they realized that he had gone over a cliff. When N.F. did not reappear, his companions shouted loudly, but received no response. Visibility improved slightly and they set up a rappel and looked over the edge. They realized the seriousness of the drop and could not see N.F. They attempted to use the radio on a number of occasions over the next few hours to report the accident but were unable to make contact with anyone. They attempted to rappel onto the slope from the Col but due to cornice conditions and the difficulty of reversing the rappel they aborted this attempt. They made a number of other attempts to get to N.F. by various routes. S.F. had the most first aid training, and he entered the slope from the south where it was marginally safer and made his way to N.F., about two hours after the fall. S.F. determined that there was nothing that he could do to assist N.F.

It was obvious from the laceration that N.F. had fallen directly on his head. There was a fair amount of blood loss from this injury. When S.F. reached N.F., he was not breathing, was cyanotic, and had no carotid pulse. (As a side note, S.F. had set off at least two avalanches in his approach to N.F. and thus chose to exit to the north of the Col, which took him through an icefall, which he then crossed solo.) One of the group skied part of the way down to him so that they could come back through the crevasses roped up. The group spent the night at the Scott Duncan Hut, where they again attempted unsuccessfully to call for help on the radio. The following day they exited at West Louise Lodge and reported the incident to the RCMP. Storm and whiteout conditions continued for seven more days. N.F.'s body was recovered by a team of Parks Canada Wardens from Lake Louise and flown out by helicopter on April 19. N.F. was buried in 80 cm of snow but his companions had taken a reading on his location. He was wearing a transceiver which made it possible to locate him very quickly.

Analysis

Whiteout conditions at the Balfour High Col are fairly common, and this is the second such incident at this precise location. The decision to unrope in good visibility at this point is common, as most of the crevasses on the way to the Neil Colgan Hut can be avoided. Since the party was not familiar with the terrain in good visibility, they likely underestimated the cornices and steep terrain to their left. The main error was in failing to remain roped up and utilize proper glacier travel techniques. The recommended way to travel on glaciers is to rope up as the "default" position. Exceptions can be made, but being in a whiteout, in unfamiliar terrain, is not one of the exceptions. Worse yet, we seem to be seeing people using "not roping up" as the default position and roping up when they sense an exception, which in turn gives "human error" an even greater chance of success.

Ski mountaineers traveling the Wapta traverse should be equipped with a compass, topo map and GPS where possible. Having a pre-marked route plan is important as well, as it is easy to make errors in navigation in difficult conditions. (Source: Greg McDonnell, Parks Canada Warden Service, Gord Irwin, Edwina Podemski)

FALL ON ROCK, PROTECTION FAILED—ROCK BLOCK, FAILURE TO TEST HOLD
Alberta, Jasper National Park, Hidden Valley

On May 19, Peter R. (49) and Jack W. were climbing a single pitch route in Hidden Valley, a quiet climbing area east of Jasper. While leading, Peter decided to sling a large block to use as protection. When weighted, the block pulled out and Peter fell about 20 feet onto a scree slope, tumbling down to a point level with his belayer. His first piece of protection prevented him from falling any further; however, the large block fell on and crushed his right ankle. After making him as comfortable as he could, his partner ran down to the road, 40 minutes away, and phoned Parks emergency dispatch. Park Wardens responded on foot to the accident scene, where they stabilized the patient and splinted his foot. Another Warden and a Jasper Medic flew into the scene and evacuated the injured climber by helicopter sling rescue to an ambulance waiting at the road.

Analysis

Rock quality in this part of the world can be quite suspect at times, especially on climbs that do not receive a high traffic volume. There is ample shattered limestone at the bottom of a number of the routes in Hidden Valley to provide clues about the rock quality in the area. Climbers would do well to visually inspect chosen natural protection carefully before weighting it. (Source: Parks Canada Warden Service, Jim Mamalis, Edwina Podemski)

FALL ON ROCK, INADEQUATE BELAY, EXCEEDING ABILITIES
Alberta, Jasper National Park, Morro Slabs

On June 22, a family group and friends were climbing at Morro Slabs, a low angle practice area near the road, east of Jasper, Alberta. The group was being supervised by the father of the accident victim. Some of the party were climbing on top-ropes, while others were practicing rappelling. One of the rappellers, Jacob (20), who was relatively inexperienced, was being belayed from the top of the climb on a separate line by a friend, who was using a figure 8 on his harness. The belayer was positioned between the cliff edge and the rappel anchor, but was not tied in to the anchor and did not have a helmet or shoes on. The rappeller was descending too quickly for the belayer to keep up, so he was pulled off the top of the slab and over the edge of the climb. He fell 60 feet to the base of the slabs.

The accident was witnessed by a passing motorist, who phoned into the Parks dispatch. Wardens quickly hiked into the site and stabilized the patient, who had suffered minor lumbar spine injuries and various scrapes and bruises. More wardens flew in by helicopter and evacuated the patient via helicopter sling rescue system to the road.

Analysis
The belayer should have been properly tied in to the anchor point, and should have been wearing a helmet and shoes. A belay directly off the anchor, or at least redirected through the anchor using the appropriate device, would be preferable to belaying directly off the harness in this case. Better communication between the rappeller and the belayer would also have helped. It is remarkable that the victim did not suffer more severe injuries given he was not wearing a helmet and the length of fall. The rappeller and especially the belayer were inexperienced. (Source: Parks Canada Warden Service, Jim Mamalis)

STRANDED—OFF ROUTE, INADEQUATE RESEARCH, EXCEEDING ABILITIES
Alberta, Waterton Lakes National Park, Crandell Mountain, Tick Ridge
A group of 25, including five teacher/leaders and 20 grade 10-11 students, were attempting the "moderately-difficult" scramble up Tick Ridge on Crandell Mountain. Several group members and leaders had difficulty with footing and exposure on the ascent. Upon reaching the Cockscomb Ridge, the leader decided to proceed directly down an easier-looking gully heading southwest toward the Cameron Lake Road. They continued downward through progressively steeper third and fourth class terrain until blocked by vertical cliff bands. They decided at this time (early evening) to send one stronger leader back up the mountain to gain cell phone coverage and call for help. The group was able to build a fire in a relatively safe spot, and stayed put for the evening. The stranded party was observed by rescuers just before dark, and as the reporting leader had indicated the party was safe and secure for the night, a dawn helicopter rescue response was planned. The entire party was slung off the mountain in the morning.

Analysis
While not strictly a mountaineering accident, this report demonstrates what happens when inexperienced people venture into mountaineering terrain. The route was beyond the abilities of several members and leaders within this large group, some of whom had no previous experience with exposure in the mountains. As well, the group leader had not been on the route before and had chosen to attempt an unknown descent line. (Source: Parks Canada Warden Service, Brent Kozachenko)

STRANDED—SOLO CLIMBING, CLIMBING UNROPED, INADEQUATE EQUIPMENT/CLOTHING, WEATHER
Alberta, Peter Lougheed Provincial Park, Mount Brock, Southwest Face
C.F., set out on July 2 around 1400 to do a solo, ropeless climb on Mount Brock, about 50 kilometers south of Canmore in Peter Lougheed Provincial Park. He told his roommate, J.S., he might head to Mount Brock and joked that if he wasn't back in two or three days, "to call someone." It was hot and sunny. He carried a chocolate bar, two hard candies, two liters of water, a guidebook for the route, a topographical map, helmet, headlamp,

sunglasses and climbing chalk. He wore nylon pants and a nylon jacket. The route he planned to climb was a moderate 5.6 pitch, which he climbed with ease after he ate his chocolate bar. At the top of the ridge, the Southwest Face of Mount Brock exposed itself, presenting "some of the best limestone I've seen," C.F. said Monday. "I decided to explore that face. I had a lot of confidence in my ability…maybe too much. I made the decision consciously. I was leaving the intended route. But I also intended not to climb anything I couldn't climb down." He spent some time exploring the face. A nice pitch of 5.7 took him to a very steep face of limestone with a corner. "When I looked at this I was pretty much blown away; it was pretty awesome, three stars for sure." He focused on the holds, the climbing. Up and down he went, executing the moves, forcing his mind to relax, enjoying what was "probably one of the most amazing climbing experiences of my life." He scaled a pinnacle, a towering rock formation similar to a hoodoo, that brought him to some shattered, broken ledges that he traversed and "in hindsight shouldn't have." Getting up and over them was one thing. Trying to back-climb them was "one of the most hideous experiences of my life." By then the sun was beginning to set, and he set his sights on the summit, planning to scramble down the other side after watching the sunset from the peak. He traveled over to another pinnacle and raced up it, thinking that there would be an easier way down the other side. What he found was an imposing wall of rock. He was only 20 feet from the summit, but the two holds he found on the rock face gave him a bad feeling. He didn't want to attempt them. Nor did he want to try to climb back down the shattered ridge in the dark. He found a small ledge about two feet wide and settled his back against the rock for the night.

His feet dangled down the mountainside, about 1,500 feet of nothing between them and the base of the face. In the dark, he heard rock trickling down the mountain and the scrabbling of claws. With his headlamp, he found the source—the huge bushy tailed wood rat or pack rat. He shooed them away and resumed his sleepless wait for sunrise. The next day he had two starburst candies and a bit of water for breakfast and continued his search for a way off the mountain. "I wanted to finish the route really bad. I read the rock, playing the moves out in my head, trying to focus on climbing the wall but the holds still deterred me. I was skeptical about committing myself to climbing back down those ridges." He did attempt them but the loose rock convinced him to go no further. Several times he got on the wall and tried to do the moves but climbed back down onto the ledge. The wind was "annihilating," burning his face. Another night passed, with a visit from the rats and hours of mental resolution. "I was trying to keep myself positive, to not be scared, to be confident. It was such a learning experience for me. I learned what my capabilities are, how to control my mind. You have to push fear aside. You have no choice."

Day three dawned overcast and cold. C.F. was cold, the rock was cold, the wind was howling. He was out of water, fighting hypothermia and losing his war with fear. The day passed much as the second had, in a frustrating search for a route off. "I just wanted to go down. I knew I was in trouble." That night it snowed, near blizzard conditions at that altitude, and his thoughts turned to his own mortality. He pulled his arms into his nylon jacket, sat on the guidebook and map, and placed his pack across his thighs. "At that point I was scared. I was hoping to God someone comes to get me. I'm thinking, 'Man, I screwed up! I'm in trouble.'" As the storm raged around him the rats came out to visit him again. "I think they wanted me to come and visit them inside their hollow pinnacle but I wasn't going to fit. They seemed genuinely concerned about me though." He also thought about his parents back in Regina. "I did the real soul searching. I started thinking about things I'd like to do before I die!" On day four he despaired. "I was fighting a mental battle not to go for those unstable holds. There were two options. I'd take a 1,500 foot fall or get over the top. The storm really beat me down. I was hallucinating, I was fighting hypothermia, my legs were stiff. I was a mess. I was going to commit myself to climbing down that day, and then the helicopter showed up."

Back home J.S. and his other roommates hadn't become concerned about C.F. until Thursday night, when he failed to show up for his shift at work. By then, there was no point in alerting rescue crews because nothing could be done in the dark. At first light Friday, they called in the alarm, and by 4:00 p.m. Alpine Helicopters pilot Lance Cooper had spotted their friend. The sight of the chopper sent one thought through C.F.'s head: "Somebody likes me." Cooper had to hover in close to the rock wall with provincial conservation officer Randy Axani dangling from the end of a 100-foot rope. Axani managed to make it to the ledge, scrabble through a rock wall C.F. had built for protection from the wind, and snapped the stranded climber into a harness. Back home, roommate J.S., one of C.F.'s frequent climbing partners has leveled an ultimatum. "He's grounded. No climbing for a week." (Source: Carol Picard, Rocky Mountain Outlook)

FALL ON ROCK, INADEQUATE PROTECTION—NO STOPPER KNOT, HASTE, INATTENTION
Alberta, Cougar Canyon, Slowpoke

"On Saturday, July 13, we gave a lesson on what happens when you vary from your normal safety routine and don't check all your gear. We were putting up a top rope on Slowpoke, a 30-meter, 5.8-rated climb with a high first bolt and a high belay station (about 15 feet above Cougar creek) for a couple friends who had never climbed outside before. D.H. grabbed my short (55 meter) rope since someone else was eyeballing the route. A moment's inattention and we both missed a critical part of our standard safety check— the stopper knot. D.H. was lowering down and had reached the second bolt when we ran out of rope and didn't have a stopper knot. He free-fell about three meters and hit his head, bounced off the cliff fell another two to three meters and hit his head and body again, then bounced into the creek to land in a pool a little less than a meter deep. He went completely limp after the first hit and was just floating once he was in the water.

"Long story short: He came around really quickly and despite a very large head wound and some initial confusion, got his bearings and started making sense pretty soon. The paramedics helicoptered him out to Canmore then drove to Calgary. After x-rays, CT scans, poking, prodding and all those other tests the final prognosis was that he is basically ok. He's just going to be really sore for a while. Oh, and the stitches come out in ten days. He's got about 80 stitches in his poor head. His doctor stated: 'If you hadn't been wearing a helmet, you'd be an organ donor right now.' He hit so hard that his helmet crushed down and cut him. D.H. feels like the luckiest man around to fall like that and be hurt so little. 'I feel so lucky that we made a mistake like that and didn't kill one of us.'" (Source: The victim's partner, Ian Greant, and Edwina Podemski)

FALLING ROCK
Alberta, Jasper National Park, Mount Athabasca, North Ridge
On August 21, Jeff (age unknown) and Andrew (33) were ascending the North Ridge (III 5.5) of Mount Athabasca. After crossing the North Glacier they ascended a short snow/ice gully to the ridge proper. While changing the rope from glacier travel mode to climbing/short-roping mode, a natural rockfall occurred. A rock hit the victim on the helmet, dazing him. The rockfall also knocked one of their ropes and a pack off the NE side of the ridge. They decide to continue, and the pair ascended short-rope style, using several tied-together slings, for several hundred feet, until the victim began experiencing a diminished level of consciousness. He could not answer simple questions from his partner, and became quite argumentative. His partner eventually managed to get him to stop and anchored him to the rock. From a ledge on the ridge, they began to call for help. A mountain guide climbing a nearby route heard their calls and notified the Warden Service using his VHF radio on the Parks frequency. Park Warden rescue parties were dispatched from Jasper and Athabasca Falls warden stations, and a helicopter was put in motion. After doing a reconnaissance flight and locating the party on the ridge, wardens were slung into the site with first aid gear. The victim was assessed and spinal immobilization was applied. Two more wardens were slung in with evacuation gear. The subject was packaged in a vacuum mattress and Bauman Bag, oxygen was administered, and he was evacuated by heli-sling to the roadside staging area.
Analysis
Rockfall is a common occurrence in the Canadian Rockies, and a significant hazard for climbers, although ridge routes such as this one are usually a relatively safer bet. Wearing a helmet undoubtedly saved the victim's life in this instance. They may have done better to take more time and assess their situation and their condition more thoroughly after the rockfall incident. It was fortunate that an ACMG guide was nearby and was carrying a radio with access to Parks frequencies. (Source: Jim Mamalis, Park Warden, Jasper National Park and R. Stephen Jobe—a climber who witnessed the incident)

STRANDED DUE TO MEDICAL CONDITION
Alberta, Banff National Park, Mount Temple, East Ridge

On August 27, while on a solo ascent of the Aemmer Couloir variation (IV 5.7) of the East Ridge of Mount Temple, W.K. started having neurological problems while ascending the couloir. He bivvied on top of the couloir and attempted to continue the next morning. He was still experiencing dizziness, and loss of fine motor control. When he became overdue, a search was initiated. Warden Service rescue crews flew him out from his location on the ridge where he was waiting for help.

Analysis

Solo climbing carries additional risks. In this case, the climber was fortunate to be able to continue to the relatively safe terrain above the top of the couloir. (Source: Parks Canada Warden Service, Marc Ledwidge)

FALL ON ROCK, OFF ROUTE, INADEQUATE PROTECTION
Alberta, Canmore, Mount Fable, Southeast Ridge

On August 28, F.L. and S.H. were climbing the Southeast Ridge of Mount Fable (Alpine II, 5.5). F.L states: " When we got to the base of the buttress, it was hard to tell where the route was, since the buttress looks like a big steep wall. So we hiked to the base of it, traversed (scrambled) right for about a rope-length and then continued scrambling up for about 25 meters. Then the route became more serious (steep rock with small holds and compact rock, but off vertical). Therefore I built up an anchor in good rock with two pieces (one nut and one tri-cam) equalized with a sling and a figure-eight knot. Before leading, I clipped my rope in the nut, which was my first piece. I started leading and climbed for two meters to a vertical rock band of about 0.5 meters. I placed a nut in a shallow crack, which didn't look so good, but was better than nothing. Then I traversed right for two meters to have a look, came back in the middle (where my nut was) and traversed left for one meter (didn't look good) and came back in the middle. The easiest climbing seemed to be on the right hand side, so there I went. The grade was pretty easy, about 5.7. (That's probably why we didn't turn back: it looked feasible!). The rock was about 70 degrees but hard to protect. I climbed the 0.5 meter vertical rockband and placed another nut in a shallow crack, which didn't look good, but again was better than nothing. I traversed left for one meter. My last pro came off just because of the rope drag. I traversed left for another 0.5 meter and as I was moving my right foot above my left, my left foot slipped (perhaps due to some sand under my rock shoe). Since the holds were quite small, my handholds were more for balance, so I couldn't hold my body weight with them and I fell.

My first and only remaining piece came off while falling, so all the force was on the anchor. I passed my belayer on her right-hand side and she stopped me. Her left hand got rope-burned. My fall was about six meters. While free falling, I bounced my right hand side once on steep rock and finally the rope stopped me. My chin was deeply lacerated and bleeding. I had sharp pain in my right shoulder, right hip and both ankles. My right hand was deeply lacerated, as well as the outside of my right ankle. I managed to stand up on my feet and S.H. lowered me for about three meters to a ledge. She undid the anchor and scrambled down to me. With my first aid kit, she made a large arm sling around my right arm and gave me another triangular for my chin. Then she covered me with my fleece and Goretex jacket. She put all the gear in the packs, coiled the rope, took my car keys, and went for rescue.

The helicopter came one hour after the call. I was lifted to Exshaw and then transported by road ambulance to Canmore." (He was diagnosed with a fractured scapula and a small pneumothorax. He will make a full recovery.)

Analysis

In the words of T.L.: "Obviously we were off route, the climbing being more difficult than 5.5. Next time, we should back-track and try to find the proper way up, not trying to climb stuff harder than the actual grade of the route." The protection which the leader thought was "better than nothing" in this case, was not. (Source: F.L., Dave Stephens)

STRANDED, POOR CONDITIONS
Alberta, Banff National Park, The Finger

On September 28, a party of two was reported overdue from a climb on the previous day. A search by Warden Service rescue crews was initiated and the party was located on the rappels on the north side of The Finger (II 5.5). They had spent the night on a small ledge. Overnight temperatures were in the –5 to –10 degree C range. The helicopter toed into a nearby ridge and a rescuer was dropped off to make voice contact with the party. They requested assistance. A party was inserted by heli-sling onto the summit and the climbers were raised back to the top. They were then evacuated by heli-sling from the summit.

Analysis

Although it is likely that the climbers could have continued the rappels down to the notch below, they were unaware that the third-class slabs below were covered in snow from early season snowfalls. It would have been very difficult to negotiate this terrain safely. (Source: Parks Canada Warden Service, Marc Ledwidge)

FALL ON ROCK, PROTECTION PULLED OUT
Alberta, Ghost River, Duveinafees

On October 8, around 1400, B.W. was leading the second pitch of Duveinfafees (5.7) when his right foot slipped while bridging and lay-backing a corner. He pulled a fixed pin, a cam (2.5 Friend) and was caught by two fixed pins slung together. He fell about 25 meters hitting a ledge in a crouching stance about halfway into the fall. He landed two meters below and eight meters to the right of the belay. He sustained a femur fracture in the fall. His partner yelled for help and proceeded to lower his partner to the base of the cliff. He then descended to the valley and drove away to get help. A party on the opposite side of valley who had heard calls could find no one at the road, so they drove down the gravel road looking for the vehicle they had seen earlier. They caught up to other climber who was having car trouble. At this point, they would have been within cell range or only a few minutes away from it. They discussed the situation and decided to go back to the site and try and move the victim down to the road. Once back at the scene, there was more discussion on moving the victim or going for help. One of them again left the scene, got in a vehicle, and, around the same location where the two vehicles had met earlier, was able to make a cell phone call. This call came in about three hours after the accident at 1700. Warden Service rescue crews responded. The patient was removed by heli-sling and flown to Banff Hospital.

Analysis

Fractured femurs are serious and considered potentially life threatening. It appears that the discussion on whether to try and move the patient rather than go for help revolved around the concern of rescue costs. They did not incur any rescue costs. It would have been very difficult to lower this patient a few hundred feet over scree and rough ground to the valley below without a stretcher. If the patient had survived this, the multi-hour trip over rough roads to the nearest hospital would likely have seriously exacerbated the situation. (Source: Parks Canada Warden Service, Marc Ledwidge)

FALL ON ICE, PROTECTION PULLED OUT—ICE TOOL
Alberta, Jasper National Park, Shades of Beauty

On November 25, three experienced ice climbers were climbing Shades of Beauty (III WI4), a three-pitch waterfall ice route in the Sunwapta River Valley of Jasper National Park. L.P. (33) had led the first pitch, and at the base of the second pitch, R.W. (35) decided to take over the lead. This second pitch has an initial 15-meter section of steep ice. R.W. led up this for about two meters and was preparing to place his first ice screw. He hooked his tool behind a chandelier feature in the ice and upon weighting it to replace his other tool, it pulled. He fell about two meters to a sloping ice ramp at the base, where his crampons dug in while his body carried forward and sideways, resulting in serious fractures to both ankles. R.W. ended up sliding past the belay to the lip of ice at the top of the first pitch, where he was stopped by L.P.'s belay. L.P. quickly constructed an improvised rope rescue system to haul R.W. back up to the belay stance. Parks Canada wardens were quickly notified by radio, and an immediate rescue response was initiated.

A Park Warden was slung in by helicopter with first aid and heli-evacuation gear. R.W.'s ankles were splinted and he was slung out to the roadside staging area, where Jasper paramedics were waiting. After initial treatment there, he was flown to Banff hospital and eventually transferred to Calgary hospital, where he underwent surgery the next day. It is estimated he will take several months to recover.

Analysis

R.W. was very familiar with this climb, as this was his third time there this season. He is also a very competent and experienced ice climber. Haste may have played a role in this accident. It is possible the hook placement of the ice tool was not weighted and tested before he pulled out his other tool. The constantly changing nature of the ice may have also been a factor. R.W. may have been successful with hook placements the week before, but on this day (a cold one) the hardness of the ice may have made a similar placement less secure.

FALL ON ICE, INADEQUATE PROTECTION
British Columbia, Golden Canyon, Lady Killer

On March 11, while leading the first pitch of Lady Killer (II W13), A.M. fell after placing three screws on the first half and then running it out to the top. He fell to the ground and sustained pelvic and spinal injuries. Volunteer SAR groups from Golden responded by ground and treated the patient. Since the injuries were severe and lowering the patient problematic, assistance was requested from the Warden Service of the National Parks nearby. The patient was evacuated to an ambulance below by Heli-sling by Warden Service rescue crews.

Analysis

Even on easier angled ice, topping out on a pitch can have disastrous results if no protection is available. In this case, the climber pulled out both his tools and was severely injured. (Source: Parks Canada Warden Service, Marc Ledwidge)

SLIP ON SNOW, CLIMBING UNROPED, UNABLE TO SELF-ARREST, INADEQUATE EQUIPMENT
British Columbia, Selkirk Mountains South, Mount Billy Budd

On August 18, J.C. and G.H. departed from a climbing camp located on north side of Houston Lake on a "day off" hike to Houston Pass at about 1200. J.C. was a very experienced mountaineer with between 20 to 25 years experience. The two climbers were outfitted with mountaineering boots and ski poles, but had no rope, helmet, crampons, ice ax, or climbing gear. Upon reaching the Pass, J.C. and G.H. followed the south-east ridge from Houston Pass that went over the Vere Summit to the summit of Billy Budd. The climbing was uneventful and was enjoyed immensely by J.C. and G.H. as it was a beautiful day. After resting at the summit of Billy Budd, J.C. and G.H. started their descent to the Houston Lake camp with J.C. in front, basically following the route of the previous day's Mount Billy Budd climbing teams. They initially followed tracks across a glaciated section (crevasses easily identified and navigated around) and then scrambled down on rock outcrops. About 1815, mid-way down the descent, at a point about 250 to 350 vertical meters above camp, J.C. and G.H. stepped off a rock outcrop to again follow tracks, this time on a traverse of a northwest-facing snow patch. Within a few steps onto the snow, J.C. slipped and started sliding down the snow which had a pitch of 45 to 50 degrees. J.C. had no ice ax, was unable to self-arrest, and slid 300 meters on the snow—and then tumbled 20 meters onto the rock at the bottom.

Several members of the group went to the accident site. It was apparent that J.C.'s chances for survival were slim. On August 19, J.C.'s body was recovered by Alpine Helicopters.

Analysis

It is unclear why the climbers would choose to cross glaciated terrain unroped and why they carried neither crampons nor ice axes whilst choosing to be on snow slopes with an angle of 45 to 50 degrees as described. J.C. was found to have died from severe head injuries. It is unclear whether a helmet would have made a difference in the outcome in this case. It is also unclear whether the ability to evacuate the victim immediately by helicopter would have made any difference to the outcome given the injuries described. (Source: Greg Hill)

SLIP ON SNOW—UNABLE TO SELF-ARREST
British Columbia, Selkirk Mountains, Palisade Mountain

On August 19, two members of a week-long climbing camp based at the Great Cairn Hut were descending the north side of Palisade Mountain on intermittent snow slopes. Around 4:30 p.m., and approximately 200 meters above the glacial valley floor, D.M. was walking sideways across a 35-degree, 20-meter-long snow slope when his foot slipped. D.M. tried to self-arrest with his ax but failed. He accelerated down the snow slope, hit a medium sized boulder at the end of it and continued to tumble over rock talus for a further five meters. M.E., who had been descending through the adjacent scree and boulders, reached him quickly and immediately carried out a thorough primary assessment, administered required first aid, and spent time ensuring that D.M. was comfortable while discussing the options of what to do next. It was clear that D.M. had a serious hip injury and that a helicopter evacuation would be required. D.M. was also experiencing some problems with breathing on his left side, and minor internal injuries were suspected even though his ribs appeared to be unbroken. M.E. hurried on to the Great Cairn Hut to summon help, arriving around 5:30 p.m. A satellite phone rented for the camp was used to call Alpine Helicopters in Golden.

The rescue team and their equipment had to be slung in on a long-line from a staging area at the bottom of the slope. D.M. was stabilized with a body air splint and prepared for helicopter evacuation. The crew and patient were in flight for the Golden hospital by approximately 8:00 p.m.

After full x-rays of his neck, spine, ribs, and hip, and failure to relocate his left hip into its socket, D.M. was transferred to the trauma center at Foothills hospital in Calgary. The dislocation movement had broken the hip joint and there were also a number of bone chips. D.M. now has a permanent plate to hold everything together. He also had some slight cracks in his lower back vertebrae and required some fluid drainage from the left lung area.

Analysis

D.M. subsequently noted that he had moved down steeper snow slopes further up the mountain and had negotiated lots of similar slopes in the past. He remarked that he tried to self-arrest with his ax but that it was pulled from his hand in the first moments and he was trying to grab it again. He felt that he was not complacent about the slope but he didn't anticipate losing hold on his ax or the speed of his slide. This illustrates the need for climbers to consider various factors in moving in the mountains: potential hazards, the ability to react and respond in the event of an incident, the potential consequences of an accident, and accident prevention through route selection and adapting technique. In this case, D.M.'s inability to self-arrest quickly along with the snow slope's short length and lack of run-out resulted in a serious crash into the rocks below. While he might have gone down through the rocks instead, this has its own hazard and moving down snow slopes is often a tempting faster alternative. However, had D.M. traversed the slope by facing more into it and holding his ax in more of a self-arrest position, he may have been in a better position to self-arrest more successfully.

This accident happened on the second day of a week-long fly-in camp and so the satellite phone was invaluable in evacuating D.M. in a timely manner. D.M. was wearing a helmet and thus did not suffer more extensive injuries. (Sources: D.M. and Marcus Eyre)

FALL ON ROCK, CLIMBING ALONE AND UNROPED
British Columbia, Dowler Range, Mount Dougie Dowler

N.S. (25) departed around noon on November 26, from Quadra Island by boat and landed at the most easterly of three creeks on the south side of Bute Inlet to attempt a solo climb of Mount Dougie Dowler (6,363 feet) in the Dowler Range on Bute Inlet, about 40 miles north of Powell River. The trek into the base of the mountain follows the creek and some fairly steep terrain likely requiring some bushwhacking. N.S. had left instructions with a friend on Quadra Island to get in touch with his family if he was not back within several days. He did not, however, leave details of the route he intended to take—only his destination.

On November 28, the friend contacted family as instructed. The first search was initiated by the auxiliary Coast Guard out of Campbell River, who quickly located the boat N.S. had left at the creek mouth. With no indication he had returned to the boat, it was decided to launch a search. Campbell River Search and Rescue became involved, and a helicopter was requested from a nearby logging company. On Nov. 29, the body of N.S. was located from the air in a snowfield. The site was about 1,000 feet below the summit and a fairly exposed and long climbing route. It was apparent on initial investigation that N.S. died after a fall of some distance, possibly from near the summit. The initial coroner's report indicated that he fell at least 800 feet and that equipment failure was not being considered as a cause.

Analysis

With no witnesses, it is not possible to say how this accident happened. It is included because it illustrates the additional risks in climbing alone and unroped. (Source: Paul Walton—B.C. Coroner's Service, *Nanaimo Daily News*, and Jed Williamson)

AVALANCHE, ICE ANCHOR FAILURE—FALL ON ICE
Baffin Island, Auyuittuq National Park, Mount Breidablik

On July 8, after reaching the summit of Mount Breidablik, a group of 14 began descending their route of ascent. They had climbed the prominent glacier visible from Summit Lake at Pangnirtung Pass. The snow and ice slope is 45 degrees at its steepest. In order to facilitate the descent for such a large group, the party fixed their climbing ropes with screw-anchors every 50 meters. The last climber would down-climb and pull the ropes and anchors as he descended. The lowest climber was waiting at a two-screw anchor when an avalanche released from above. The avalanche hit the lowest climber and the anchor failed. He was swept 200 meters down-slope and suffered a broken leg in the fall. The victim was stabilized by a doctor in the group and one member descended to the Park Warden Patrol Cabin at Summit Lake. Fortunately, a Medium helicopter working in Qikiqtarjuaq (Broughton Island) was available and dispatched to the accident scene. The helicopter was able to land nearby and the patient was evacuated to Pangnirtung. Fixed wing aircraft then flew him to the hospital in Iqaluit by Nunavut Health Services. (Source: Parks Canada Warden Service, Marc Ledwidge)

EQUIPMENT FAILURE THROUGH IMPROPER USE—INADEQUATE ANCHOR
Québec, Sageunay National Park, Cap Trinité, Les Grands Gallets (5.9, A2+, 350 m.)

A couple began their planned three-day outing to climb Les Grands Gallets at Cap Trinité on Saturday August 4. They were seen climbing around 100 meters up on Les Grands Gallets (5.9, A2+) on Saturday. On Sunday, park rangers became alarmed when they could no longer spot them on the rock face. Their bodies were found in a crevice at the foot of the cliff. Police believe L.P. and J.V. fell between 100 and 150 meters to their deaths, some time between Saturday and Sunday. The two had intended to spend the night in a portaledge. L.P. had previously acknowledged to a newspaper reporter that she was nervous about sleeping in the portaledge, for it would her first time using such equipment.

Analysis

A public inquiry determined that the fall occurred while the couple were resting on their portaledge. The couple had overloaded their portaledge with too much weight, had improperly attached it to their anchor system, and had neglected to tie themselves in to an independent anchor. (Source: Tu Thanh Ha—*Globe and Mail,* and Edwina Podemski)

FALLING ROCK, WEATHER
Yukon Territory, Mount Augusta, North Buttress

At 1500 on June 18, South District Ranger Daryl Miller in Talkeetna, AK, was phoned by Charlie Sassara's wife, Siri Moss, about an accident on Mount Augusta—a border peak 20 miles northeast of Mount St. Elias on the U.S.-Canadian border. In the U.S. the land is managed by Wrangell-St. Elias National Park and in Canada by Kluane National Park. Jack Tackle (40's) and Charlie Sassara had flown onto the Seward Glacier at 6,300 feet on June 16 in order to attempt a new route on the North Buttress (Canadian side) of Mount Augusta. After caching their skis at 7,700 feet the pair began climbing on June 17 in the early morning.

At 2000 on the 17th, after 12 pitches of climbing, the team began looking for a suitable bivouac ledge at 9,200 feet. The first ledge they chopped proved too small for the tent so at 2200 Tackle climbed to a higher ledge to investigate its suitability while Sassara belayed. About 60 feet up, Tackle was excavating a possible ledge when a briefcase size rock struck him in the back causing him to fall. The protection that he had placed held and Sassara arrested his fall quickly. The blow initially paralyzed Tackle. Sassara was able to lower Tackle directly back to the existing ledge and secure him to the belay. Tackle's pain was so severe in his chest and abdomen that Sassara feared internal injuries. Sassara was able to stabilize Tackle in two sleeping bags inside the tent and secured him to the mountain using both rock and ice protection. Sassara remained on scene throughout the night helping Tackle with fluids and making him more comfortable. The team discussed their options and concluded that a helicopter rescue was Tackle's best chance for survival because they feared that lowering him could have been fatal.

Sassara began descending at 0630 on the 18th. It took him 13 rappels and five hours to reach the glacier and then another 45 minutes to ski to their base camp where they had a satellite phone. Sassara called Kluane National Park and his wife to notify them of the emergency.

Kluane's Chief Park Warden Ray Breneman and Hunter Sharp (Assistant Superintendent of Wrangell-St. Elias National Park) worked out a memorandum of agreement for cross border rescue cooperation. Miller offered to gather a ground team of experienced climbers and RCC offered air support. The Canadians had a helicopter capable of short-haul operations at these altitudes and were getting ready to fly to the scene. Miller assigned the mission to ranger Joe Reichert, who located Kelly Cordes, Colby Coombs, and Michael Alkaitis to form a ground team and emergency hired them. At 1930 the four flew from Talkeetna to Kulis AFB, Anchorage where they boarded a C-130 to Yakutat, Alaska. Arriving in

Yakutat at 2200, the NPS team conferred with the PJ's who had flown down on the Pavehawk. After discussing the options, the Pavehawk launched to locate the climbers on the north side of Mount Augusta and see if they could perform a rescue that evening. Because of poor weather, the pilot opted to not take additional personnel at that time. Unable to see either climber due to clouds and poor lighting, the helicopter returned to Yakutat at 2340 after locating skis at the base of the mountain face. Due to darkness, the operation was suspended until morning. The helicopter remained in Yakutat while both crews returned to Anchorage.

While this staging and reconnaissance was taking place, the Canadians were trying to get to the scene but due to low clouds and the VFR capabilities of their aircraft were not able to get closer than 50 miles to the site. The weather did not improve enough for VFR aircraft until June 20.

On the 19th, a C-130 returned to Yakutat at 1000. At 1130, the Pavehawk launched with three crew members, two PJs, and Reichert on board. Arriving on scene at 1215, Tackle's tent was located during the second pass and his elevation was determined to be 9,200 feet. Charlie Sassara could not be located at the team's basecamp due to clouds below 8,000 feet. The helicopter continued to make reconnaissance flights until the C-130 was in the air providing communication and fuel support for the mission. Once the C-130 was on scene and the fuel load was down to levels that maximized the helicopter's power, the first hover was made on location. All power checks were positive, so the pilot slowly guided the aircraft closer to the mountain above the tent while Reichert and PJ Robertson were estimating clearance distances for the pilot. PJ Shuman was lowered on the winch about 140 feet before he started swinging. Unable to stop the oscillations, the ship pulled away from the cliff, ending the first attempt. Another hover reconnaissance was made before the final lowering.

On the third trip hovering above the tent, all personnel were familiar with the site and their role in the operation, so it proceeded more quickly. Shuman was able to get on the ground below the tent, hike up 20 feet to the site, open the side of the tent and attach Tackle to the hoist cable. The engineer took up the slack and began to hoist as the pilot flew clear of the cliff. As Shuman and Reichert tended to Tackle, the helicopter crew met the C-130 and refueled while returning to Yakutat. Both aircraft were on the ground in Yakutat at 1430. In Anchorage, Tackle was taken by ambulance to Providence Hospital.

Charlie Sassara waited at his base camp until June 21 when he was flown out by helicopter, as softened snow conditions and crevasses prevented a fixed-wing evac.

Tackle was found to have several broken vertebrae. The extreme pain that he had in his chest and stomach was apparently due to bruised nerves in the spinal column. Tackle's specific injuries were a broken T1, broken T4-T5, and minor fractures in T8-12. He had a bruised spinal cord and impinged nerves at T8 and T10. He also had three broken teeth and major cartilage and intercostal tissue breakage in the sternum area of the front lower rib cage, as well as a severely bruised left shoulder.

Analysis

Tackle was climbing this last section without his pack because he was only scouting for a campsite. The weather was also a contributing factor. The temperature was 15 degrees F when they started to climb and it unexpectedly warmed up during the day, which probably contributed to increased rockfall. (Source: Joe Reichert, Mountaineering Ranger)

(Editor's Note: For a first-hand account of this incident, see the magazine Alpinist I, *Number 1, 2002)*

Charlie Sassara received the David Sowles medal from the American Alpine Club, which is in recognition of an individual or individuals who give of themselves in an extraordinary manner to provide aid to climbers in distress.)

UNITED STATES

FALL INTO CREVASSE, CLIMBING UNROPED
Alaska, Alaska Range, Idems Peak

On March 24, Karoline Frey (27), a German graduate student at the University of Alaska, Fairbanks, died after falling 90 feet into a crevasse while snowshoeing down a glacier about 45 miles south of Delta Junction.

Martin Stuefer was one of three friends on the ski trip Sunday with Frey. Stuefer said the group decided to ski and snowshoe to the summit of Idems Peak. They made it up easily and retraced their steps back down. "There was no sign of danger when we went up," he said.

Frey was leading the way down when the snow gave out, Stuefer said. She fell through an opening about three feet in diameter hidden by a snow bridge. Stuefer said he and the two others in the group, Tim Dennenbaum and Tina Din, could see no sign of Frey after she fell.

"I looked down the crevasse and I couldn't see the bottom. We cried down and we never got an answer."

The group had neither cell phone nor radio. Leaving Dennenbaum and Din at the scene, he skied down the mountain, drove to Pump Station No. 10 of the trans-Alaska oil pipeline, and asked workers to call for help.

Troopers initially responded in a helicopter but were unable to land on the glacier. At 9:30 p.m., the Alaska National Guard landed, found the body, but were unable to recover it that evening. The Alaska Mountain Rescue Group resumed the recovery effort Monday.

Frey was buried beneath several feet of ice and it took four hours to dig her out, said Soren Orley of the rescue team. (Source: From an article in the *Anchorage Daily News* by Anne Marie Tavella, March 27, 2002.)

Analysis

It is not a good idea to travel unroped on a glacier, especially if one is not familiar with it. (Source: Jed Williamson)

AVALANCHE–BACKCOUNTRY SNOWBOARDING, POOR POSITION
Alaska, Mount St. Elias

On April 7, John Griber was carefully working his way down a 45-degree ice face on Mount St. Elias. He turned at the sound of a "swish" above. Forty to 50 feet away, he saw companion Aaron Martin (32) off his skis on his side and sliding. Griber watched for 30 seconds as Martin slid hundreds of feet and out of sight. Then the snowboarder yelled for the second skier in the party, Reid Sanders. There was only silence.

Pilot Paul Claus of Ultima Thule Outfitters in Chitina on Friday reported spotting a body about 3,000 feet below the peak, with a string of equipment tracing the route of a fall. Claus, a noted Alaska Bush pilot, planned to return to see if a body recovery was possible. Griber and a fourth climber, Greg Von Doersten, were rescued by a National Guard helicopter Wednesday.

Below is part of Griber's conversation with The Associated Press by telephone.

Griber said the men intended to climb the mountain, then become the first to ski or snowboard to sea level from such an elevation. Martin and another team had tried the same thing a year earlier only to be turned back by blizzards. This year the weather was sunny, calm, and relatively warm in the days after Claus dropped the men off at Hayden Col, a pass just above 10,000 feet, on April 4.

The next day the climbers tackled their first hurdle, a sheer 3,500-foot ice face. Climbing with 65-pound packs stuffed with food and gear for a higher camp, the four ran into a problem when Von Doersten lost a crampon on the last pitch, preventing him from climbing. By the time Martin pulled him up on a rope, Von Doersten had frostbitten his hand. The climbers dug a camp into the snow near 14,500 feet. Von Doersten decided to stay there while the others went on.

Griber, Martin, and Sanders set off the next day and by Sunday had reached 16,000 feet. The next morning, they were ready to go for the summit but faced another ice wall. It was not as steep as the first, Griber said, but the surface was lined with channels a few inches to 15 inches deep caused by water melting, flowing, and freezing. By late afternoon, though, the men were above that headwall and within 600 to 700 feet of the summit. Griber rested there while the others pushed forward.

"I just felt really drained," he said. "I wanted to let them take advantage of not pulling me up."

Griber estimates he paused 10 minutes, then followed the footprints of the two skiers. At 6:15 p.m., 150 feet from the summit, he decided he could go no farther. He worried that it would take another 20 minutes to the top, and darkness was coming.

Griber took off his crampons and neoprene overboots and locked into his snowboard. In severe conditions, Griber said, he often snowboarded with an ice ax in his hand. This time, he had one in each hand. "This wasn't snowboarding," he said. "This was absolutely survival technique." Still, he noted the conditions were the same or better than the three had encountered on previous trips.

"This is what we were used to doing," he said. "We specialize in high angle, extreme terrain. We're not just a couple guys who went out and said, 'Let's go ski this thing.'"

Griber started down. He paused occasionally, he said, to wait for Martin and Sanders. Within half an hour or less, he spotted his companions about 800 feet above. Griber slowly continued down the mountain for another 15 minutes, looking for good snow, occasionally able to make a turn. When a few ice balls rained down, he figured Martin and Sanders must be directly above. Griber said he felt it was "a little dangerous." He traversed across the slope to be out of the way if anyone fell. A few minutes later, he heard the sliding sound, and over his right shoulder saw Martin. Martin had self-arrest grips on ski poles for braking to a stop on steep snow, but he could not stop.

Griber yelled for Sanders, but heard nothing. Sanders had yet to clear an area of unstable ice columns and crevasses, Griber said. As darkness fell, Griber put on his headlamp and made his way into a band of talus and rock, where he jettisoned his snowboard. He tried climbing on the rocks, calling for Sanders, and looked for a flat place to bivouac. Eventually, concerned with his own safety, he put his crampons back on, located the footprints the climbers had made that afternoon, and walked on ice in the dark until he found a crevasse to provide shelter from the bone-chilling wind.

"I was feeling cooked at this point," he said. "I was beyond tired."

He woke at 5:00 a.m., searched again for Sanders, then descended to the old snow shelter at 16,000 feet. He stayed long enough to warm up in a sleeping bag, then descended to 14,500 feet to tell Von Doersten of the tragedy.

A day later, Claus flew over to check on the climbers. Griber and Von Doersten waved to him, and Griber used his ice ax to carve out a message in six-foot letters: "TWO DEAD." Claus dropped a weighted bag with a note saying rescue was possible, and for the climbers to raise both arms if they needed help.

"I fell to my knees and raised both hands," Griber said.

A HH-60 Pavehawk helicopter from the National Guard's 210th Mountain Air Rescue group in Anchorage came to get them. The crew had to lighten it to safely climb to 14,000 feet. Griber and Von Doersten abandoned their camp and equipment on the mountain to scramble aboard the flight to safety. (Source: Associated Press and *Anchorage Daily News* reporter Craig Medred)

FALL INTO CREVASSE
Alaska, Talkeetna Mountains

At 1700 on April 26, Alpine Ascents guide Brian McCullough (42) was traveling with three clients on an unnamed glacier in the Talkeetna Mountains when he broke through a snow bridge and fell fifty feet into a crevasse. McCullough landed at the bottom of the crevasse on his left side, his sled was caught by the rope and stopped just above him. Within minutes of the fall one of the clients approached the crevasse and determined that McCullough could ascend the rope. The clients then constructed an anchor and McCullough began ascending the rope. As McCullough approached the top, it was determined that a separate line would be necessary, as the original line had cut into the lip of the crevasse in the fall. Another anchor was constructed, and McCullough was able to ascend out of the crevasse on a separate line. After removing the rest of McCullough's equipment that had been tied to the initial fall rope, the group decided to camp for the night.

On the morning of April 27, the team traveled to a location up glacier at approximately the 8,000-foot elevation. They believed it would be possible for a plane to land there and then stomped out a runway. The weather over the next five days was a combination of heavy rain followed by snow and then high winds. On the morning of May 2, Doug Geeting went to pick up McCullough and the three clients, who were now four days over due, on the Talkeetna Glacier. Not seeing McCullough's group at the airstrip, Geeting traced the group's planned route and spotted them. Geeting attempted to land at the group's location but the snow conditions proved to be too firm to land safely and extract the injured party. He informed the group that they would have to return to the location where they had been dropped off—approximately two day's travel. The combination of McCullough's injured ribs, a potentially loaded slope on the route to the drop-off location, and the urging of the three clients, all of whom were Emergency Medical Technicians, persuaded McCullough to request evacuation assistance.

At 0905 on May 5, the National Park Service Talkeetna Ranger Station was contacted by Doug Geeting regarding an injured climber in the Talkeetna Mountains. Since the location was outside park boundaries, rangers referred the caller to the Alaska State Troopers. At 1006, the Alaska Rescue Coordination Center (RCC) contacted the National Park Service Talkeetna Ranger Station to request assistance. At 1140, the NPS Lama helicopter was dispatched to the scene with NPS Helicopter Manager Dave Kreutzer and Ranger Gordy Kito on board. At 1215, the Lama was on scene and Kito assessed the injuries as possible multiple fractured ribs on the left side. The patient denied any other pain or injuries. At 1230, the Lama departed the scene with Kreutzer, McCullough, and one client for Palmer State Airport. Upon arrival McCullough was taken to the Valley Hospital in a private vehicle and was diagnosed with nine broken ribs (3-11) and released. At 1335, the Lama retrieved Kito and the remaining two clients and transported them to Palmer.

Analysis

Crevasses are one of the inherent dangers of glacier travel. McCullough recognized the increased risks of the area in which he was traveling and tied the whole team together using two ropes. The added weight of the other members may have prevented more serious injuries. McCullough's sled was tied into the rope using a prusik and the handles on the sled duffel were also clipped into the rope multiple times. These measures are standard for glacier travel and most likely prevented the sled from landing on top of McCullough and causing further injury, as well as the possibility of the sled being lost in the crevasse. The team was able to secure the rope, assess McCullough's condition, and help him to extricate himself from the crevasse.

One contributing factor to the distance of the fall may have been the fact that the team was traveling on a 9mm dynamic (high-stretch) climbing rope. Some mountaineers are looking into using "low-stretch" (a.k.a. static) ropes for glacier travel to help mitigate the issue of elongation in a crevasse fall.

Repeatedly, the anecdotal evidence points to injuries being caused by the falling climber coming into contact with an object, whether it be the bottom of the crevasse or a ledge, and not from the force created by the rope and harness system arresting the fall. The mountaineering community may need to look into ways to stop crevasse falls in a more reasonable distance, since the dynamic properties surrounding a crevasse fall (i.e. the rope cutting into the lip of the crevasse, partners being dragged) increase the distance traveled and therefore the likelihood that the falling climber will come in contact with something.

However, the testing of low-stretch ropes for glacier travel is incomplete and can not be recommended at this time. Given McCullough's injuries, evacuating via the ascent route, which required travel through rough terrain with a heavy pack, would have been ill-advised. Given the assessment of the pilot that snow conditions were unfavorable for an evacuation by plane, the safest option was to evacuate using a helicopter. (Source: Gordy Kito, Mountaineering Ranger)

FALL INTO CREVASSE (1) AND FALL ON ICE/WINDSLABBED SNOW, INADEQUATE PROTECTION, DESCENDING UNROPED, FATIGUE
Alaska, Mount McKinley, West Buttress

On May 15, a five member Spanish expedition, "Gambo De Palamos," left their camp at 17,200 feet to attempt the south summit of Mount McKinley. Shortly after leaving, Rafael Morillas-Cabrerizo turned back due to a headache. At 1400, Enrique Llatser-Fontanet turned back because of cold hands. While descending alone from Denali pass, Llatser-Fontanet fell into a crevasse and managed to extricate himself. He walked himself back to the 17,200-foot camp and presented no serious injuries. The remaining three team members continued unroped to the summit.

About 2030, the three remaining team members reached Denali Pass and continued their descent unroped. Shortly thereafter Francisco Rodriguez-Martin slipped and fell 800 feet. Luis Ropero-Civico and Miguel Angel Romero-Ruiz continued hastily toward the 17,200-foot camp, and within ten minutes of Rodriguez-Martin's fall, Romero-Ruiz slipped and fell 700 feet. At 2130, team member Morillas-Cabrerizo alerted NPS staff at the 17,200-foot camp that he "needed a rescue." Although he did not see either fall occur, he could see only one member descending and was concerned for the others. At 2145, the two fallen climbers were spotted unmoving at 17,400 feet, and a land rescue was initiated from the 17,200-foot camp.

The one remaining climber descending, Ropero-Civico, reached the 17,200-foot camp at 2200 with no injuries. Ropero-Civico and Morillas-Cabrerizo assisted NPS staff Mik Shain, VIP Tucker Chenoweth and Air National Guard Pararescueman John Davis with bringing the two fallen climbers back to the 17,200-foot camp. Romero-Ruiz was found unresponsive and showing signs of severe head trauma. He was transported back to the 17,200-foot camp in a Cascade litter with three attendants. Rodriguez-Martin was found stumbling with no gloves and showing signs of severe chest trauma. Chenoweth and Davis cleared Rodriguez-Martin of a spinal injury, and he was walked back to camp with two attendants. Both patients were brought back to the 17,200-foot camp by 0020, on May 16.

Rodriguez-Martin and Romero-Ruiz were placed and stabilized in a tent and administered low flow oxygen. When hot water bottles were available, they were placed in the patients' sleeping bags. At 1012, Rodriguez-Martin was loaded onto the NPS Lama helicopter and flown to the 7,200-foot base camp. Romero-Ruiz was placed on a backboard and fitted with a cervical collar and was loaded onto the Lama's second trip to 17,200 feet at 1048. Both patients were transferred to the Providence LifeGuard helicopter at 1133 and transported to Providence Hospital for treatment.

The remaining team members expressed concern for Llatser-Fontanet's condition and his ability to descend to the 14,200-foot camp. VIP Dr. Michael Ross reassessed Llatser-Fontanet, finding pain associated with his right knee and left shoulder, but found no reason to grant helicopter assistance. On May 17, NPS Ranger Shain and VIP (Volunteers in Parks Ranger) Chenoweth assisted Llatser-Fontanet's descent by short-roping him to 16,200 feet. NPS Roger Robinson and VIP's Lance Taysom and Brian Okonek continued the effort by lowering Llatser-Fontanet down the fixed lines and into the 14,200-foot camp.

Rodriguez-Martin was treated and released from Providence Hospital May 24. His injuries included nine broken ribs, a flail chest, and severe frostbite to both hands. Romero-Ruiz was treated and released on May 29. His injuries included an occipital head fracture, pulmonary contusions, a right pelvic fracture, and a right tibia-fibula fracture.

Analysis

The descent from Denali pass at 18,200 feet has a long history of climbing incidents. Surface conditions are often icy and present a hazard to fatigued climbers descending from a summit attempt. Guided parties frequently place up to 20 snow pickets and ice screws as anchors for a running belay from 17,500 feet to 18,200 feet. These anchors are often left *in situ* for others to use for the season but are removed by the end of each season. No guided parties had reached the upper mountain before the Gambo De Palamos expedition made their summit attempt. Surface conditions on May 15 were very icy with a two-inch breakable wind crust. The combination of poor footing, fatigue, and a difficult surface for self-arresting contributed to the falls. Rodriguez-Martin had left his ice ax secured to his pack, making it impossible to attempt a self-arrest.

A running belay would have prevented the falls. The party had set up a running belay on their ascent to 18,200 feet but chose to remove their pickets as they climbed. Again, fatigue and the proximity to their 17,200-foot camp probably led to their descending without protection. Despite its moderate angle, the slope between 17,500 feet and 18,200 feet should be crossed with caution. (Source: Mik Shain, Mountaineering Ranger)

FALL ON SNOW, PARTY SEPARATED—CLIMBING ALONE, FATIGUE
Alaska, Mount McKinley, Denali Pass

On May 18 at 0600, Kunibert Gramlich, from Germany, stumbled into the 17,200-foot camp on the West Buttress of Mount McKinley and requested assistance from National Park Service Ranger Mik Shain.

The Swiss Denali 2002 expedition began their ascent of Mount McKinley on May 11 and arrived at the 14,200-foot camp four days later. Following a rest day, the team made a summit attempt from the 14,200-foot camp. Gramlich became separated from the others during the day and was descending alone from Denali Pass. At some point he fell approximately 30 feet and injured his left side. To his credit Gramlich made it through the night alone without incurring environmental injuries, but upon his arrival at the ranger tent, he succumbed to exhaustion and spent the following ten hours in an NPS tent as volunteer doctor Mike Ross evaluated him. Doctor Ross discovered tenderness along the left chest wall and a large bruise below the rib-line. Ross was most concerned about the contusion on the soft lower left side that could indicate a life threatening injury of the spleen. Gramlich was administered oxygen and warm water bottles in an NPS sleeping bag. Rangers Reichert and Shain wanted to give the patient some time to stabilize to see if he could recover to the point where he could walk down under his own power. Following his initial assessment, Dr. Ross felt it could be dangerous for Gramlich to descend because another fall could cause his spleen to rupture.

The Swiss Denali 2002 expedition members who were at the 14,200-foot camp were notified and several of the team decided to ascend to see if they could help. Ranger John Evans was told that one of the ascending party was the "team doctor." The teammates arrived at 17,200-feet between 1300 and 1400 and Dr. Ross conferred with the "team doctor" for a patient assessment. At that time Ross discovered that the person was a doctor of geology and that medicine was his "hobby." Based on the pain that Gramlich experienced when sitting up or trying to walk, his low blood oxygen saturation (54% off of oxygen) and the mechanism of injury, Dr. Ross, with Rangers Reichert and Shain, decided that Gramlich needed a helicopter evacuation. At 1515 the request was made to Talkeetna, and at 1730, Gramlich was flown from 17,200-feet to 7,200 feet.

From the base camp at 7,200 feet on the Kahiltna Glacier the patient was flown to Providence Hospital where Gramlich spent three days. He was diagnosed with several lower left rib fractures, a small spleen laceration and a bruised liver. He was treated for pain and held for observation. No surgery was necessary and he was released on May 22 to local lodging in Anchorage where he was to rest and check in with the doctor one more time before returning to Germany.

Analysis

The Swiss Denali 2002 expedition should have traveled together and roped up. The leader, Richard Bolt, should not have allowed Gramlich to travel alone after the rest of the party descended. Because the fall was not witnessed, it is not known what caused it. Fatigue, icy conditions, and lack of concentration because camp appears so close are all contributing factors to accidents on this slope. (Source: Joe Reichert, Mountaineering Ranger)

HAPE, HACE, CLIMBING ALONE
Alaska, Mount McKinley, West Buttress

At 1813 on May 27, Joshua Wax (28), a solo climber experiencing symptoms of high altitude cerebral edema (HACE) and high altitude pulmonary edema (HAPE), was evacuated by helicopter from approximately 18,800 feet on Mount McKinley's West Buttress route. The National Park Service Lama helicopter short-hauled Wax to the 7,200-foot base camp where he was assessed and transferred to a fixed wing aircraft, which flew him to Talkeetna. Wax was then transferred to a Lifeguard helicopter and transported to Providence Hospital in Anchorage.

Analysis

Solo climbing has inherent risks. Although Wax was advised not to solo by many people, including the park rangers, he made that choice. It is believed that Wax left the 17,200-foot camp on the afternoon of May 26 for the summit. The details of Wax's ascent are incomplete. It is believed that he was descending from the summit when he became disoriented and ataxic. He is thought to have collapsed on the "football field" late night on the 26th or in the morning of the 27th.

As Wax climbed higher and started to be affected by high altitude cerebral edema (HACE), his judgment became impaired and his decision-making capacity became diminished. If Wax had a partner with him, he/she may have noticed these changes and encouraged or convinced Wax to descend. This may have avoided putting additional climbers and National Park Service employees and resources at risk. Wax was incredibly fortunate to have been found by a passing party and equally fortunate that they had the knowledge, skills, and ability to effect his rescue. Had Wax not been found he surely would have perished. (Source: Gordy Kito, Mountaineering Ranger)

FALL INTO CREVASSE, DISTRACTING ILLNESS, UNSEASONABLY WARM WEATHER
Alaska, Mount McKinley, West Buttress

An Alpine Ascents International guided party led by Forrest McCarthy descended from the 14,200-foot camp on May 27, after their climb on the West Buttress. While descending the standard route on the Kahiltna Glacier, client Derek Joynt (33), fell into a crevasse at the 6,800-foot level at approximately 1900—half mile from the base of "Heart Break Hill." The party of seven was traveling roped wearing snowshoes in one team of four and one team of three, with Joynt roped in the middle of the three-person team. McCarthy led the first team of four while guide Eric Remza led Joynt's team. As Joynt fell in, he shouted, "Falling!" Remza and the third roped member Kirt Mayland went into self arrest. There was no indication of the crevasse, which ran parallel to the trail. Joynt fell in to where only his head was observed. McCarthy turned his team around and quickly set up a 2:1 pulley system to extract Joynt. Joynt slipped further into the crevasse because this first rescue attempt was parallel to the crevasse, causing the rope to slice further into a soft temperature-gradient snow.

Joynt began to complain of becoming very cold as he was unable to remove his gear. The TG (temperature-gradient) snow slowed down the process of placing anchors and preparing the crevasse edge. After realigning the anchor system to be perpendicular to the crevasse, a 3:1 pulley system was started. Immediately upon raising, Joynt complained loudly that he was experiencing pain after his right snowshoe became wedged in the crevasse. This operation was stopped and Remza descended into the crevasse to give aid to Joynt. Remza removed Joynt's sled and pack and then assisted Joynt out of the crevasse. Once out, Joynt was found to be scared and very hypothermic experiencing pain in his right hip area. The concern that Joynt had a potential hip injury prompted McCarthy at 2100 to request assistance from the NPS at basecamp. Ranger Roger Robinson received the call where a hasty team was assembled led by Ranger Scott Metcalfe. In the mean time, Remza treated Joynt's hypothermia while McCarthy probed the area for crevasses and set up a fixed line for rescuers to work from.

Metcalfe's team arrived on scene at 2120. At 2130, Dr. Chad Page, VIP of Metcalfe's team, requested that Joynt be evacuated by helicopter. Page felt that Joynt had sustained possible pelvic and hip fractures that needed immediate attention. Joynt was administered morphine and Percoset along with being placed in MAST Pants. At 2257, the NPS Lama helicopter evacuated Joynt to Talkeetna with Ranger John Leonard as the attendant. Joynt was then transported to the Valley Hospital by ambulance where he was released on May 28.

Analysis

Some of the warmest weather recorded occurred the last two weeks of May causing a significant melt cycle to occur in the Alaska Range. This created unseasonably hazardous conditions for lower glacial travel. The AAI party was descending with a climber who had experienced altitude problems higher on the mountain. Once they reached the 7,800-foot level at 1500, they decided to continue on toward basecamp, as this individual continued to show signs of AMS. Their minds were focused on him, even though the traveling conditions on the glacier were poor the further they descended. If they had waited at 7,800 feet until the early morning, they would probably have been able to descend to basecamp without mishap. (Source: Roger Robinson, Mountaineering Ranger)

FATIGUE—PULMONARY INFECTION, DEHYDRATION, INADEQUATE EQUIPMENT—NO STOVE
Alaska, Mount McKinley, Direct West Buttress

At 2121 on June 2, Jim LaRue (45) and River Lee-Elkin (27) of the "NW Buttress 02" expedition, after spending over forty hours on the Direct West

Buttress, were assisted (including providing water) by National Park Service volunteer Wayne Fuller and Ranger Gordy Kito.

On May 15, LaRue and Lee-Elkin flew into the Southeast Fork of the Kahiltna Glacier to attempt the Northwest Buttress of Mount McKinley. They climbed to the 14,200-foot camp on the West Buttress to acclimate before heading over to the Northwest Buttress. At 0800 on May 31, LaRue and Lee-Elkin departed the 14,200-foot camp to attempt a new variation of the Direct West Buttress. The route ascends from the 12,500-foot basin, just below "Windy Corner" on the West Buttress, to the top of the "fixed lines" at 16,200 feet on the West Buttress. The pair left an itinerary with Mark Givens of the "Colonial Mountain Militia" expedition. Their expected time en route was twelve to eighteen hours.

When interviewed LaRue and Lee-Elkin stated that they believed the route would take just over 12 hours. As they approached the top of the route, LaRue became short of breath. He had taken over an hour to second pitches. Late on the night of June 1, the pair decided to spend the night out and finish the route in the morning. After a sleepless night, they climbed toward the top of the route. Approximately 50 feet below the top of the route, LaRue became concerned that his breathing difficulty may have been high altitude pulmonary edema. The pair decided that their safest option, rather than traversing the ridge at 16,000 feet, was to rappel the route in order to lose altitude more quickly. Rappelling the route, over 30 pitches, took the majority of June 2.

LaRue was examined by NPS volunteer Doctor Jennifer Dow. Upon examination, Dow found a possible pulmonary infection that worsened with altitude and exertion. LaRue had a productive cough with green sputum and no blood. LaRue's condition improved slightly with the administration of an Albuterol inhaler. After several days at the 14,200-foot camp, LaRue and Lee-Elkin decided to return to the 7,200-foot base camp.

Analysis

The team was dehydrated and extended to its limit. It is believed that this team would have been able to return to the 14,200-foot camp without the assistance of the NPS, but their safety margin would have been stretched rather thin. LaRue and Lee-Elkin reported that they thought they made a mistake in not bringing a stove to melt water. Other than this oversight the team was well prepared and encountered an unforeseen medical condition. It should be noted that LaRue and Lee-Elkin had previously traveled to the 17,200 foot camp to leave a cache without any altitude related illness. (Source: Gordy Kito, Mountaineering Ranger)

AVALANCHE, POOR POSITION, WEATHER
Alaska, Mount Foraker

On April 6, the Talkeetna Ranger Station received mountaineering registration forms for Kevin Strawn (27), Travis Strawn (21) and Colby Strawn (15). They intended to climb both the West Rib on Mount McKinley and either the Southeast Ridge or Northeast Ridge on Mount Foraker. Ranger

John Leonard reviewed their registration forms and found their prior experience adequate for their planned routes. The two older brothers had climbed Mount McKinley in 1999 and all three had numerous ascents in Alaska with other ascents including Mount Rainier and the Grand Teton. Leonard signed off on the review, and the leader, Travis Strawn, was sent our NPS mountaineering confirmation letter dated April 16. No other formal contact was made until their arrival in Talkeetna.

On June 8, the three brothers checked into the Talkeetna Ranger Station where Ranger John D. Evans conducted the briefing. As reported by Evans, "They had obviously done a lot of research into the route on the Southeast Ridge of Foraker; however, they were open to alternative routes and ideas if their planned route was unsuitable once they got into the mountains to assess it. Other routes discussed included the Sultana Ridge of Foraker and the West Rib of Denali. Also discussed during the briefing were assessment of snow conditions and different tactics in attempting the routes. Overall my assessment of the team was that they were an experienced team whose members were approaching a potentially serious climb with clear heads and a lot of information."

Ranger Joe Reichert also visited with the Strawn brothers. Reichert stated, "In my conversation with the Strawn brothers on June 8 prior to their check in with John Evans, we spoke of the possible conditions that they might find on the Southeast Ridge of Mount Foraker. I mentioned that it had been attempted twice early this season, once in March and once in May. Both parties found deep faceted snow and decided to retreat from low on the route. Then we spoke of possible current conditions. I told them that there had been significant new snowfall in late May and early June. I stated that this could stabilize the poor winter snow pack, but that it could also pose high avalanche hazard due to the heavy new snow over the weak layer. We visited some about life endeavors since I had checked them in for a previous Denali expedition. We parted with my usual farewell to climbers: Have fun and climb safely."

After a weather delay, PJ Hunt of Doug Geeting Aviation flew the three to the West Fork of the Kahiltna Glacier on June 11. This glacier is the start for the Southeast Ridge route on Mount Foraker. They took 18 days of food for their possible two climbs with a return date no later than June 27. That evening at 2030, the Strawn brothers called the Kahiltna Basecamp and spoke with the manager Lisa Roderick via CB radio. They asked her if she would contact their wives concerning a bag of climbing equipment that had been forgotten. This equipment would be needed for their climb on the West Rib of Mount McKinley. The message was relayed to the Geeting Aviation office. Apparently the bag could not be located.

On June 12 in the early evening, Hunt flew over the ridge to check on the three and spotted their camp at the 8600-foot level on the South Toe of the Southeast Ridge. One person waved to him at that time. A little later in the evening the brothers again called Kahiltna Basecamp to check on the status of their bag of climbing equipment. Roderick reported that the brothers thought the bag was left with Geeting Aviation. Roderick told them that she would continue to check on its whereabouts.

On May 12 at 2030, the Strawn brothers called into basecamp and spoke with Roderick. Roderick stated that "they sounded concerned about conditions of the route." In their call they indicated they had been climbing on shale and hinted there had been some rockfall. They reported they were at 10,000 feet and going further that evening. Roderick read them the weather report that indicated a possible clearing trend. In signing off they said "they would check in at 0830 with me [Roderick] every night" since they were unable to hear weather forecasts from the 14,200-foot camp. After their climb on Mount Foraker, they asked Roderick "to hold the bag [if found] and they would pick it up for their West Rib climb." Roderick stated "they did not indicate when" this date would be.

No other radio transmissions were heard from the Strawn brothers after the 13th.

On June 17 at 1537, the Lama helicopter departed Talkeetna with Ranger Robinson—who had initiated a search, Helicopter Manager Dave Kreutzer, and Pilot Jim Hood. Weather was clear and calm at 1610 when the Lama reached the 7000-foot level of the South Toe of the Southeast Ridge of Mount Foraker. The brothers' cache of skis was observed at the base of the ridge at the 6500-foot level. Continuing up the route, tracks between snow and shale could be observed along the ridge crest above 9000 feet. At 10,000 feet the tracks in the snow were followed traversing a 30-degree slope below an ice headwall. Wands with orange flagging were placed on this traverse. The traversing tracks led through avalanche debris to the broken rock buttress that forms the Southeast Ridge proper. Faint tracks were observed above the avalanche debris ascending several hundred feet up a 45-degree ice rib paralleling next to the rock buttress. From near the 10,500-foot level, the tracks appeared to be a single faint set stopping short of a small fracture line that spanned the ice rib. The fracture appeared to be less than six inches in depth.

Robinson directed the Lama to continue the search up the Southeast Ridge reaching 14,500 feet at 1620. The search continued to 16,000 feet with no other evidence so the Lama descended to the last known location at 10,500 feet. Robinson directed the Lama to begin a slow descent down the fall line from this last know spot. Between 10,000 and 9,500 feet, several wands were observed lying on the 45-degree ice and shale slope. A significant amount of surface melt water and a few small rocks were observed cascading through this area. Directly down the fall line at the 8500-foot level at 1635, the Strawn brothers were found deceased and spaced apart on their rope. They were on a 35-degree slope and it appeared they had been lying at this location for several days as the surface snow had melted away except what was under their bodies. Pilot Hood felt he could retrieve the three with the "Grabber," so the Lama headed for Talkeetna. At 1829, the Lama departed Talkeetna en route to the basecamp with Hood, Kreutzer, Ranger John Evans, and Helicopter Mechanic Ray Touzeau arriving at 1906. At 1920, the Lama extracted the brothers using the Grabber and flew them back to basecamp. At 1928 the three were positively identified by Evans and this was relayed to Talkeetna. Hunt flew the remains of the Strawn brothers back to Talkeetna where they were transported by vehicle to Kehls Mortuary in Palmer.

Analysis

The Southeast Ridge of Mount Foraker has a record of both avalanche fatalities and victims of avalanches that have survived. Unfortunately, the section of route the Strawn brothers encountered was in a high-risk avalanche zone that has proven to be difficult to assess. Most of the lower routes in the Alaska Range were reported to be in poor condition when the three flew in. Waiting for a good settled period of weather before climbing higher was really the only safe option at that time.

In further observation of the accident site, it appeared the lead climber triggered a very small soft slab avalanche. This person may have been able to regain his footing though the avalanche carried at least one or both of the other brothers down the slope. This momentum made it impossible for the lead climber to hold the fall. Their faint tracks were visible after the avalanche slid because they were kicking in steps that penetrated the older snow layers. The avalanche slid on one of the newer snow layers allowing the tracks to remain. (Source: Roger Robinson, Mountaineering Ranger)

FALL ON SNOW, UNBELAYED, EXHAUSTION
Alaska, Mount McKinley, West Rib–Notch Camp

At 1430, on June 18, Russ Watts (33)—from Italy, fell 150 feet from the Notch Camp on the West Rib. Watts reported that he was investigating the snow conditions on the West Side of camp when he slipped on icy conditions and tumbled toward the 14,000-foot basin between the West Buttress and the West Rib of Mount McKinley. Watts team members, Kimi Johnson and Peter Hodum, descended to the slopes where he lay. He did not lose consciousness but was not able to walk. Hodum and Johnson, trained in wilderness medicine, assessed his injuries and called Ranger Scott "Scooter" Metcalfe by citizen's band radio. Metcalfe, based at the 14,200-foot ranger camp, recruited rescuers among the National Park Service volunteers and mountain guides who were at the 14,200-foot camp. Johnson and Hodum reported that Watts had right rib, left shoulder, right hip, and back pain. The two teammates assembled a makeshift litter with skis, foam pads, sleeping bags, and rope and began to lower him toward the 14,200-foot camp. In three rope teams, the rescuers ascended toward the West Rib, carrying ropes, pickets, a SKED, medical equipment, and other rescue gear.

At 1745, the NPS rescuers reached Watts position at approximately 16,200 feet. The rescuers set snow anchors and constructed a lowering system consisting of a main line and a belay line. Dr. Chad Page performed a preliminary assessment of Watts while in the litter on a snow platform. He was alert and oriented. He had significant right rib tenderness, left scapula tenderness, and left pelvis and femur tenderness. He was able to move and feel his hands and toes. He did not have neck or head pain. He was given 30 mg of Toradol in his right shoulder muscle and three Percoset tablets. He was given the tablets because the morphine vials that were carried to the site were empty. The plungers which hold the morphine had apparently fallen out, allowing the morphine to exit the back of the vial. Watts had moderate to severe pain in his left pelvis when he was moved. Watts and his improvised litter were placed in a SKED. The improvised litter appeared to be sturdy but did not completely support his head and neck. He had relief of his pain with the medicines. He did not complain of pain or cold during most of the lowering. The SKED eventually reached a lower angle slope at approximately 14,500 feet from where he was carried to the medical tent at the NPS camp at 14,200 feet. Watts was transferred to a padded cot with full spinal immobilization. He was carefully undressed. Both Dr. Chad Page and Chief Brian Gerard of the US Navy performed a complete physical examination.

On the morning of June 22, Watts was flown to Alaska Regional Emergency Department. He was later x-rayed and diagnosed with 21 fractures to include one femur, one shoulder, ten transverse processes of the spine, and nine ribs.

Analysis

Russ Watts failed to have a belay while he checked snow conditions out the door of his tent at the 16,200-foot Notch Camp on the West Rib. He was exhausted from a previous ascent to the summit the day before. Watts attempted to make a scuff test of a small cornice to check snow conditions, but the snow released causing him to fall approximately 150 feet. (Source: Scott Metcalfe, Mountaineering Ranger)

FALL IN RIVER, PACKS TOO HEAVY, MISPERCEPTION
Alaska, McKinley River

My three pals and I (25, 25, 35, 39) were visiting Denali National Park with plans to climb Mount Brooks. The approach features a ford of the McKinley River. The river is a mile wide in all, but quite braided. Most of the braids can be simply splashed through, but some are quite serious.

We left Wonder Lake Campground at midnight on June 18 and hiked to the river. We began the ford at about 3:00 a.m. under the awesome alpenglow illuminating the entire Wickersham Wall. Obviously the river was cold and the current strong. We were lined up single file facing upstream inching across from our left towards our right. We reached the crux of the crossing a little more than half-way across the river. The person in the front decided it would not go and that we were to inch back the way we came. Soon mayhem was upon us.

Most of the riverbed is rocks, but there are sand and gravel areas. As we started back I stepped onto a gravel area and the riverbed washed out from under me. Quickly I went from a standing position to a kneeling position in the river. I knew immediately that I could not stand back up with my backpack on, so I jettisoned the pack into the river. Everything got very hectic and I'm not certain of ensuing details. Moments later I was swimming with Marie and her pack. She and I managed to swim and crawl to a sandbar and drag her pack out of the water.

As Marie and I stood up on the sandbar, we saw Todd on his back floating downstream on top of his backpack! I shouted to him to let the pack go but he said he could not. Moments later he was able to turn over and swim and drag himself to a sandbar just downstream from us. Cory was the only one able to stay upright, and he successfully waded to the sandbars. First he checked on Marie and me, then went to aid Todd. Led by Cory, the team was able to get back to shore. We watched as my backpack floated downstream, around a corner, and out of sight.

Todd, Marie and I were cold, shivering uncontrollably with teeth chattering. Todd and I had suffered contusions and harsh abrasions on our swelling knees from fighting and crawling up onto the sandbars. We set up the one tent we had left, gathered our wits, and licked our wounds. The air temperature was quite warm so our hypothermia was of short duration.

Later Cory and I hiked downstream and spotted my backpack, run aground on a gravel shoal. It was, of course, on the other side of the river. We spent hours fording the river to reach the pack. Upon reaching my pack Cory pointed out that we had, indeed, reached the opposite side of the McKinley River. We divided the load and forded, again with adrenaline but without further incident, back to the south shore and our emergency campsite.

After regrouping, we decided not to try the river again, but instead to backpack around and up the Muldrow Glacier. We were not successful in reaching Mount Brooks, but we did explore the rugged north side of the Alaska Range.

Analysis

First, our packs were too heavy. We had considered it a point of style that we would carry all our gear from Wonder Lake to McGonnagal Pass rather than hiring a dog sled team to move some gear during the winter. Having made that decision, we then decided to ford the river in one carry. Once I was on my knees in the river, there was no way I could stand up again under the weight of my backpack. (Our packs were too heavy, and when we attempt this again we will halve the weight in our packs and perform two carries.)

Second, we had been surprised to see a group of four climbers coming out of the mountains. They successfully forded the river at the place where we attempted. Thus we did not spend much time looking for our own crossing place, but decided that since they had done it there, we would try it there. (Next time I would take the packs off and explore, possibly for hours, looking for just the spot that our group, not some other group, could cross.)

Third, all of us had our pack belts undone, so it should have been easy to ditch them. However Todd was using trekking poles, as we all were, and when he attempted to ditch his pack he realized that he was wearing the wrist loops. Thus, in the bedlam he could not extract his arm from his backpack shoulder strap.

We had practiced fording rivers before leaving home (Washington state) and had found a method with which we were comfortable. Some will question our method. I think our method was reasonable.

We continued hiking even though Todd and I suffered injuries to our knees. Despite swelling and pain, we enjoyed a big hike into the heart of Denali. Unfortunately this resulted in Todd tearing the cartilage under his kneecap, which, months later, would require surgery.

Despite the accident and following hardships, we agreed that the trip was a success in that we kept it together, covered some beautiful ground, and thoroughly enjoyed each other's company during our visit to Denali National Park. (Source: Christopher Kemp)

FALL ON SNOW, CLIMBING ALONE, EXHAUSTION
Alaska, Mount McKinley, Denali Pass

On June 19, a solo climber from Canada, Michael Heck (61), of the "Whitevale" expedition flew onto the Southeast Fork of the Kahiltna glacier to begin a climb of the West Buttress. On June 28, Heck arrived at the 17,200 foot camp on the West Buttress, and the following morning he departed for the summit. At 2200 on the 29th, word was passed from the 14,000 foot camp to Rangers at the 17,200 foot camp that a guided party had encountered Heck as they where descending from the summit. At the time Heck was continuing his ascent above the "Football Field" at 19,500 feet. Heck, in a brief conversation with the guided party, stated he was going to continue onto the summit, and, "If I don't return by 0600, send the rangers to look for me." At 0005, on the 30th, Heck was spotted at Denali Pass. Rangers at the 17,200-foot camp began to monitor his decent and observed that he was traveling in normal fashion. At 0035, NPS Patrol member U.S Navy Chief Brain Gerard observed Heck begin to fall from the traverse just below Denali Pass to a point at which he came to rest about 17,100 feet.

After notifying Talkeetna, Park Ranger John Leonard assembled a hasty-team that consisted of NPS Patrol members Brian Gerard, Matt Hendrickson, and himself, the three then proceed to Heck's location. At 0230, park rangers reached Heck, and at 0236, Heck was pronounced dead.

After difficult flying conditions for several days, it finally became possible to recover Heck's body on July 10.

Analysis

This incident has many of the components of a classic Mount McKinley accident. Heck, who was a solo climber, was descending after a long and tiring summit day. The terrain he fell on is considerably steeper and more exposed than he had just traveled on above Denali Pass. In addition, Heck had said that he "was not in shape for the climb." In conversations with Heck prior to his climb, rangers tried to convey the seriousness of what he was about to undertake. Due to his lack of recent glacier experience, Rangers tried to convince him that it would be best to climb with at least one other person. However, he was unable to find a partner and so decided to continue as a soloist. Unfortunately, since Heck was traveling unroped, he was unable to use any sort of protection that might have been able to help arrest his fall. Heck was one of five unroped climbers that had to be evacuated from above 17,000 feet in 2002, and was the first fatality on Denali since 1998. (Source: John Leonard, Mountaineering Ranger)

HIGH WINDS AND POSSIBLE AVALANCHE
Alaska, Mount McKinley, Harper Glacier
On the evening of July 3, a 16-member National Outdoor Leadership School (NOLS) expedition was hit by high wind or possibly debris from an avalanche at approximately 17,200 feet on the Upper Harper Glacier. Although no members of the party were injured in the initial incident, a substantial amount of gear was lost and some students ended up with mild frostbite. The group spent two nights at the 17,200-foot camp before descending to 15,100 feet on July 5. The group was resupplied at 15,100 feet on the Harper glacier by the National Park Service contract Lama helicopter at 1400 on July 7. The entire group descended to Wonder Lake without further incident after receiving an airdrop resupply of equipment and food.
Analysis
With no evidence in the way of debris or actual visualization of an avalanche, it is hard to determine the exact cause of the tents' collapse. A wind event accompanied with suspended solids, i.e. snow either being transported off the ground or from an upwind event, will have a much higher density and therefore a much larger impact on the objects in the winds path. Even if there are few suspended solids, gusts of wind often blow down snow walls at the 17,200-foot camp just over Denali Pass on the West Buttress route. It is not unusual for groups to use bamboo wands as a sort of "rebar" to strengthen snow block walls or to even build walls that are two-blocks thick in order to prevent walls from blowing over.

The Upper Harper Glacier is much more exposed than the high camp on the West Buttress route, and teams should be aware that during any wind event they will be exposed to the direct force of the wind with little chance of using terrain for shelter. The wind high on Mount McKinley has left many teams fighting to survive and has been the cause of several fatalities. (Source: Gordy Kito, Mountaineering Ranger)

(Editor's Note: The last accident is actually what is called a "near miss" in that no serious injury or damage occurred. It is included because of it's educational value regarding the Harper Glacier approach, which is now used by few climbers except for NOLS. This organization has been using this route annually—and without incident—for many years.

There was one other fatality in Alaska. In late July, Marc Springer (30) was part of a four-member team attempting the Devil's Thumb, a 9007-foot peak about 120 miles southeast of Juneau. Springer fell to his death sometime during the night, according to his partner. Weather was a factor, but there were no other details.)

LOOSE ROCK CAME AWAY—FALL ON ROCK, FAILED TO FOLLOW INSTINCTS
California, Sugar Loaf

On January 12, Jon Hanlon and I were enjoying a fabulous winter day of rock climbing at Sugar Loaf. We spent the morning on a couple of the area classics, and at lunch decided that we would ascend the east chimney, a 5.7 route that had been added to the list of recommended climbs in the last couple of guidebooks. Despite my 31 years of climbing at Sugar Loaf, this was a route I had never attempted. The climb is two pitches and is tucked away in an alcove below the world famous Grand Illusion. I led up about twenty-five feet of steep rock without placing protection. When the angle backed off, I climbed another fifteen feet or so to a flake where I placed my first cam.

The climbing proceeded easily along a low-angle ledge to the base of the chimney where I placed a #3 Camalot. I remember moving up the chimney and thinking, "This really requires 5.7 chimney moves." About ten feet higher, I placed the second piece: a #3-1/2 Camalot. I moved up another ten to twelve feet to two large wedged chalkstones. As I moved past these, I placed my hands on top of them. Immediately the inside chalk stone rolled and forced my left shoulder back until there was a "pop." The chalkstones, at this point, fell straight down the chimney and knocked me off the rock. I came to a stop about fifteen feet below the highest piece of protection. The chimney was clean, so I did not hit any other objects. The lower piece in the chimney pulled out, and, when the rocks were falling, I noticed them hitting the rope, and I had the fleeting fear that somehow they would sever the rope.

The impact of my weight falling on the rope, however, caused it to snap around the rocks, and while it was frayed, it did not break. After the rocks stopped on the low angle section 20 feet above the ground, I paused to take stock of my condition. I called to my belayer that other than my ankle, which had been hit by the rock and was bleeding profusely, I was okay. Jon lowered me to the ground. We managed to stop the bleeding by wrapping it with the sleeve of a shirt, and I was able to limp out to the car. We proceeded to the Marshall Hospital in Placerville, where I received ten stitches for the gash in my foot and was diagnosed with an avulsion fracture of my right fibula.

Analysis

I felt very lucky that I was not under the rocks when they fell. I was also fortunate to be able to walk out to the car unaided. The accident, perhaps, could be chalked up to an error in judgment. After decades of looking at this chimney and concluding that there was no good reason to go up there,

I let the fact that it had been recommended in a couple of guidebooks cause me to ignore the fact that it is just an ugly old chimney climb. (Source: Bart O'Brian)

FALLING ROCK, POOR POSITION
California, Mount Shasta, Avalanche Gulch

On June 8, I (Tim Derouin) was climbing up Avalanche Gulch on Mount Shasta with Mike Chase and his brother Steve. The weather over the past few days had been quite unsettled and very windy. The previous day almost no one made it to the summit because of the high winds. The weather was getting better, but it was still windy. We left Horse Camp (7,800 feet) at about midnight and reached Helen Lake at about 4:00 a.m. We continued on and were on schedule when I was hit by a falling rock at about 5:00 a.m. at 11,2000 foot elevation. This is above Helen Lake but below the prominent rock formation known as The Heart. The rock must have dislodged from above us and bounded down the steep (25 degrees) snow slope. There were no parties above us. Because I had a hood on and was bundled up to keep out the wind, I never saw or heard it before it hit me on the right shoulder. The next thing I knew I was tumbling and sliding down the snow but managed to arrest myself or come to a halt after about 50 feet. Not sure which rock hit me, but we think it was the size of a softball. There was extreme pain in my shoulder and initially I thought it might have been dislocated. My climbing partners rushed to my aid, and after determining that I was not in shock and had no life threatening injuries, Steve raced down the mountain to summon help while Mike and I finally decided the best thing to do was rig up a sling and start hiking down the mountain. Waiting for rescue by helicopter or rangers would only mean sitting in the cold for hours. And since I seemed to be able to walk okay, the best thing was to get down as fast as possible and get medical attention.

At Helen Lake there is a ranger tent that is always up during the summer climbing season and Mike and I decided to stop there for a rest. However, inside was a ranger intern. We woke him up and he was able to call down on his radio and accompany us to the trailhead—a three hour walk—where an ambulance was waiting to take me to the hospital. There they took x-rays and the doctor gave me the good news (no dislocation or serious ligament /tendon damage) and bad news (distal third fracture of clavicle). After four weeks in a sling, physical therapy, etc., I am pretty much back to normal now.

Analysis

I learned several important lessons from this experience:

Lesson #1: Always wear a helmet! I was wearing one and was thankful I did. In addition to the shoulder injury, I had a gash below my right ear from a blow that caused some temporary hearing loss due to fluid/blood in that ear. The thinking is the gash may have been caused by the rock glancing off my helmet before it hit my shoulder. Not sure, but either way, if the rock had hit me in the head without a helmet, I might be in very bad shape.

Lesson #2: Always be prepared for rockfall! Avalanche Gulch has the highest exposure to rockfall on Mount Shasta but we had tried to minimize the risk by climbing earlier in the season and early in the day. Sometimes that is not enough. I should have been a little more observant through the Helen Lake to Red Banks section as well as that is where rockfall is most likely.

In conclusion, my fellow climbers and Mount Shasta rangers were great! Mike and Steve were a great help and comfort in getting me safely to the trailhead, as was the ranger intern whose name escapes me. The rangers even retrieved a couple of day-packs that we left at 11,300 feet when the accident happened and got them back to us. (Source: Tim Derouin)

(Editor's Note: There were several other incidents on Mount Shasta, most of them similar to those reported over the past few years. Only one or two narratives from this area will be reported each year.)

FALL ON ROCK, INADEQUATE PROTECTION
California, Yosemite Valley, El Capitan

On the morning of May 26 Thaddeus Josephson (20) and I, (Ben Mathews—26) were starting our fourth day on Sunkist (VI 5.9 A4) on El Cap. Thaddeus polished off pitch 14, the spectacular A3-4 pitch shown on the cover of Don Reid's *Big Walls Guidebook*. As I cleaned it I was glad to see that good pro could be found every ten to 15 feet. I would get my first ever A4 lead on the next pitch and could deal with it if I got the same protection. But when I reached Thaddeus's hanging belay, the 15th looked very thin and scary, and we both realized that it would be a serious lead.

I started up at about noon. Thaddeus sat facing the wall, belaying me with a Grigri clipped to his harness and with my end of the rope running through his left hand. The first piece was a bolt five feet left of the belay and just right of the crack. The seam was the thinnest I had ever seen, so I clipped a Screamer to the bolt to reduce the impact on the system if I zippered the pitch.

My first few moves were on RURPs (Realized Ultimate Reality Pitons) and beaks, then a tied-off and sawed-off angle, barely body weight. Then more RURPs and beaks and a cam hook. Then the seam dissipated to nothing and I was forced to make my first-ever head placement except in practice, knowing that if it failed so would everything else.

After almost two hours I was 35-40 feet above the belay, on another beak. A rivet ladder beckoned, only two moves away, but those were beak moves and I had only one left. I was really gripped. I placed my last beak, the most marginal piece yet, and weighted it. I realized I needed the beak below me and gave it a slight upward tug. Even that was too much for the top piece. I heard a "pop" and was in the air. "Ting, ting, ting," went the iron as I zippered the entire 40 feet. I hit the wall a few times, tumbling—and glad, in retrospect, that I was wearing a helmet. Thaddeus went by as a blur, then I was dangling upside down, grabbed the rope and righted myself.

Thaddeus yelled down and I replied, mostly on adrenaline, that I was fine, but by the time I'd jugged to the belay, I could tell that something was not right in my abdomen. My stomach felt bloated and painful and that scared me a lot, wondering what I'd done to my insides.

Thaddeus was trembling. He'd been yanked sideways two or three feet toward the bolt despite being tied in snugly, but more significantly, rope had shot through his ungloved left hand. It was badly burned and essentially useless.

We set up the portaledge and yelled for help, and in about 30 minutes the rangers contacted us by loudspeaker. We were only able to understand half of their yes/no questions due to the wind and Valley noise, but eventually we communicated and by 4:30 p.m. a helicopter began flying the rescue team to the top. It seemed as though hours went by. I was getting extremely cold and losing feeling in my left leg, in addition to the pressure in my abdomen and sharp pain in my lower left ribs.

With the sun getting low, we realized we might be spending the night on the wall, but then a rescuer with a litter came over the edge a few hundred feet above us. That's when it hit me that the risk I had accepted for myself on the route now involved many others. It took a bit of work to get me from the portaledge to the litter but we made it. The hardest part for the team may have been carrying me all the way up the slabs from the rim to the summit. We made it by a little after midnight. I was cold, wrecked both mentally and physically, and frightened by what my injuries might be.

We bivvied on the summit. In the morning my lower abdomen was numb and hard. I was loaded on a helicopter at first light, flown to the park helibase, then to Modesto. After all sorts of tests, it turned out that I had fractured three lower ribs on my left side. My abdomen had suffered "only" massive muscle and connective tissue damage and my internal organs had escaped injury. (Source: Ben Mathews)

Analysis

Despite belaying with a Grigri, enough rope ran through Thaddeus's hand to burn it severely. The Screamer may have made things worse, because as it extended downward, it lowered the angle of the rope exiting from his hand, increasing the downward pressure on his skin. But don't skip the Screamer next time, and (don't forget to) add the gloves!

Flipping upside down isn't the best way to stop: it doesn't allow the stopping force to be distributed properly by the harness and there's a greater likelihood of hitting something. Ben was wearing a chest harness, but only as a gear sling. There are ways to rig the chest and seat harness together that allow the falling climber to stop upright and stay that way. There are also dangerous ways to rig them, so seek competent instruction!

But even a chest/seat harness rig won't keep you from tumbling during the fall, and a lethal head injury is possible even on a wall as steep as Sunkist. Follow Ben's example—wear a helmet. (Source: John Dill—NPS Ranger, Yosemite National Park.)

FALLING ROCK—FALL ON ROCK
California, Yosemite Valley, Middle Cathedral Rock

On June 2, John Kurth, 33, and Casey Shaw, 39, were climbing the Direct North Buttress (17 pitches) on Middle Cathedral Rock. Shaw led pitch 15 at about 6:00 p.m., following a chimney. Twenty to 30 feet before the belay, he came over a lip to find three rock slabs piled on top of each other on a small, sloping ledge. All were large—with the the top one at least three feet by six feet, and almost two feet thick—and they looked precarious. He snuck by them on the right, yelled to Kurth to be careful, and continued up the pitch to the belay. Kurth, almost a full rope-length below, didn't hear the warning.

As Kurth approached the ledge, his right side into the chimney, the angle of the pitch hid the upper two slabs from his view. He reached up and pulled on the bottom one, not realizing the danger. Instantly he and Shaw heard the grinding of rock on rock as the whole pile collapsed. The bottom piece shot by him on the left; the middle one literally landed in his lap, but it miraculously wedged itself into the chimney at the same time, so it only pushed him off his stance. The top slab slid out and over his head, smashing into his helmet and left shoulder as it passed. He fell five to ten feet down the pitch until stopped by Shaw's belay. He immediately felt severe pain in his left arm and almost instinctively raised it to a more comfortable position over his head. Below him he could see the top slab still skating down the wall. A party behind them had retreated some time earlier and he realized that they might have died had they stayed on the route.

The rope had somehow survived the passage of all three rocks and now lay underneath the wedged piece. It was trapped but still running free. Kurth stayed where he had fallen, braced in the chimney, with his left arm over his head. He was afraid that if he lost consciousness he would weight the rope, bringing down the remaining slab.

Shaw tied off the belay and lowered a loop of the lead line over the top of the slab. Kurth tied in, then untied from the end so that Shaw could retrieve it. With tension from Shaw, Kurth was able to get to a safe resting position above the slab and about 20 feet below the belay. Shaw tied him off and rappelled to him. Kurth's shoulder was swollen and extremely painful and he couldn't lower his arm—they both had emergency medical training and worried that his shoulder was not only dislocated but completely pulverized. Potentially more serious, the back of his neck hurt as well.

They considered whether to rappel the route or continue up with Kurth prusiking, but both options seemed much too difficult, considering his pain, the possible neck injury, and the need to maintain traction on the arm. With considerable reluctance they yelled for help and soon received an answer from the Park Service over a loudspeaker. It was too close to dark to attempt a helicopter rescue, and a nighttime ground approach, intricate and loose, was equally risky. They would have to wait until tomorrow.

Shaw maintained traction on Kurth's arm all night and well into the next day, shifting the angle of the arm every 15 minutes or so to deal with spasms in the injured muscles. Kurth was able to slip on a warm jacket and with the food and water they'd brought they were as comfortable as could be expected.

In the morning the NPS tried reaching them directly by helicopter. The wall was too steep to clear the rotor blades, so rescuers heli-rappelled to a ledge two pitches above. They reached Kurth at about 11:00 a.m. and raised him, supported by one rescuer and with his neck and back immobilized. Morphine made a little difference, but not much, and all the way up Kurth had to hold up his splinted arm while fighting the pain and the confines of the chimney.

Kurth was finally short-hauled under the helicopter down to the Valley at 4:00 p.m., then flown to Doctors Medical Center in Modesto. He was found to have a fractured humerus and a dislocation of the left shoulder. The shoulder was not reduced until midnight, almost 36 hours after the accident. Despite being bashed by the rock, his head and neck turned out okay, but there is a very good chance he would have been killed without his helmet.

Analysis
Other than the obvious—Yosemite rock is often loose, and repeated warnings to the second are always a good idea—what can we say? Kurth is one very tough—and lucky—guy! (Source: John Dill—NPS Ranger, Yosemite National Park)

FALLING ROCK—FALL ON ROCK, FAILED TO FOLLOW INSTINCTS
California, Yosemite Valley, Lost Brother

On September 29, I set out with Christian Dragheim and Chris Kerr, fellow members of the Cragmont Climbing Club, to explore the Lost Brother, a seldom-visited formation on the south side of Yosemite Valley between Sentinel Rock and the Cathedral Rocks. We hoped to locate the second pitch of the 5.6 first ascent route taken by David Brower, Ruben Schneider, and Morgan Harris in 1941. Christian, Sam Tabachnik, and Christian's friend Sean and I had explored the route the previous spring but had not found the second pitch, ascending instead a strenuous 5.9 corner and lieback system, after which we retreated. I later called Morgan Harris, the only surviving member of the first ascent team, who lived in Berkeley, to ask him to describe the route. He told me in a high, quavering voice that they had climbed a series of chimneys after the first pitch. The Sierra Club Bulletin for 1941 offered a few more details, but not much. Since Morgan was well on in years, I wanted to bring him a photographic record of the climb on our return. I particularly wanted to show him that we didn't have to use a shoulder stand to get through the bulging overhang on the first pitch, as he and Brower had done sixty years ago!

The cliff band, which the second pitch ascends, appeared to have three or four chimney systems fairly close together, so we decided to try the one furthest to the left and then explore the others as time permitted. I took the lead, heading up a ramping gully to the base of the first of what appeared to be a series of chimneys separated by easier sections. I climbed through two short chimney sections and noted a fair amount of loose rock. Shortly after Christian called out the half-rope mark, I called down to suggest that he untie from the belay anchor so that he would be free to take shelter from falling rock. It occurred to me to suggest that he and Chris move off the belay ledge altogether, but for some reason I did not.

At the top of the second chimney section, the chimney flared, and I began stemming. I saw that I would have to step on a large detached block, perhaps half the size of a refrigerator, and I butted it with the heel of my hand to test it for stability. It seemed okay, and I moved up, putting my left foot on top of the block after securing a good fist jam with my right hand. As I weighted the rock, it tipped over and fell, and I had a flash of terror as I flailed in space with my feet, trying to stay above the collapsing block and the cascade of rubble spilling out behind it. I was very fearful both for myself and for Christian and Chris below. The next thing I remember was sliding headfirst down the chimney/gully, nothing in my vision but the dust, leaves, and sticks immediately in front of my face. I remember jolting down over the rock, waiting for the rope to pull me tight, and wondering why it was taking so long. Then I felt the rope catch, and I found myself just a few feet above the belay ledge, with one of the two ropes cinched tight around my right thigh and my breath coming in short, painful, moaning gasps. I croaked, "Slack, slack," to get Christian to relieve the pressure of the rope on my leg. Still tucked under cover to avoid the cascade of rocks, Christian was incredulous at hearing my voice just a few feet away. Looking up, he saw me hanging above the belay.

He couldn't get any slack out of the rope, however, and didn't want to pull it because it was caught up in a tangle of loose rock above. He also couldn't undo the knot on my harness because it was under the tension of my weight. Chris asked if he had a knife and Christian told her to dig his Swiss knife out of his pack while he clipped me in to an anchor. She handed it to him and he cut the rope at my harness, finally allowing me to slide to the ground while he helped me down. The ledge was narrow, so Christian had some trouble controlling me as they lowered me. I asked him to take off the gear rack, which was gagging me, and the huge cams on the back of my harness, which were digging into my back, and then he and Chris tried to make me as comfortable as possible, obviously very concerned by the pain I was in. There was almost no place for me to stretch out, and they finally managed to squeeze me in behind a small tree after bending the branches back. I realized the pain I was experiencing was from broken ribs and could feel the bone ends grinding together in my back when I moved or when my back muscles went into spasm, which occurred every so often. I tried lying down but found that I was only comfortable sitting up. I also had a slight but sharp pain in my left hip and figured I probably had a hairline fracture there as well.

The fall had ripped off the low-cut climbing shoe on my right foot, which was badly scraped and bleeding. The left foot didn't look much better. I asked Chris to get my hiking boots and socks, which I had left at the belay, and put them on my feet. I then noticed that the back of my right hand was pretty well shredded and the skin on many of my finger tips on both hands was scraped off, and a little flap of skin was sticking out on my cheek. While a lot of things were oozing, nothing was really bleeding badly, however. My helmet was still on, and Christian said it had no big gouges or scrapes on it. As I started to get my breath and the pain subsided somewhat, I realized that I was going to be ok, and that I was very lucky. The broken ribs made it very painful to move, so Chris and Christian made me as comfortable as they could, then wrapped me in the mylar space blanket I always carry in my epic kit. I had never been in one before, and it was surprisingly warm. I also asked Chris to get my wool balaclava and nylon windbreaker out of my pack and put them on me and then put my helmet back on. I have always considered these two pieces of gear to be well worth carrying for emergencies, and they proved it on this occasion.

Christian gave Chris his first aid kit, which had some codeine pills in it, one of which Chris later gave me. Christian then discussed how he planned to get down, saying that he would rap the route. I gave him my car keys and emergency whistle and asked him to blow it when he got down to the road, so we would know he had gotten that far, although we never did hear it. As he left, I was suddenly very grateful to have two climbing partners.

Christian cut off as much of the rope as he could get and started the descent scramble. After going a short distance, he decided that the descent we had taken the previous spring would be faster, so he traversed over to a fixed rope that some other climbers had rigged for getting up to a project. Finding a second rope there, he borrowed that to rig to the belay tree, since the portion that he had cut off my rope was too short. When he reached the road less than an hour later, he flagged down a group of passing motorcyclists and asked to use a cell phone. Dialing 911, he was put through to the Highway Patrol, which put him on hold for five minutes. Finally, he was put through to the Yosemite duty ranger and asked for a rescue.

Meanwhile, Chris and I sat and watched as low clouds moved into the Valley, obscuring the upper half of El Cap. Anxious and not enjoying my own thoughts, I asked her to talk to me about her life, and she did, describing the ups and downs of her work and home life. It was a relief to be thinking about somebody else's life at that point! We sat there for about three and a half hours while the clouds continued to move in, always remaining above us fortunately, for I was sure if they lowered we would be shrouded in freezing mist. Scattered raindrops "fwapped" on the mylar space blanket, but we were lucky in missing the pelting downpour that hit the upper valley. Occasionally, Chris fed me bits of food and held the water jug to my lips while I sipped. I found that my right arm was pretty much immobile because of the pain in my ribs, although my left arm worked fine.

I discovered that my Lexan water jug, which I carry on my harness, had been ripped off in the fall and the lid had completely disappeared. My camera, which was in a carrying case clipped to my harness, had also disappeared. The gear loop on my harness where it had hung was ripped open. Chris also showed me one of my carabiners she had found on the belay ledge. It was a wire gate with a deep gouge in the metal of the spine. The gate was crushed and twisted and lay immobile against the outside of the gate head. How it had opened and closed again, with the wire gate ending up outside, was a mystery.

I had taken the fall at about 1:15 p.m. and Christian had left at 1:40 p.m. From about 3:00 p.m. on, we watched the road anxiously, looking for cars parking along the pavement. A few showed up, and we figured they had to be members of the valley search and rescue team. About 5:15 we heard voices, and members of the team began to appear. The first one I saw was tall, skinny, and wore a tattered cap, and I somehow knew he had to be the redoubtable Werner Braun, although I had never met him before. When he ignored my greeting I was perplexed at first, then recalled he was very hard of hearing. He secured the remaining rope with a clove hitch, and then I heard him up behind me drilling a bolt for a lowering anchor.

Keith, the EMT, bent over me and asked me a bunch of questions, took my pulse and shined a little light into my eyes. The team members managed to get me into a litter and then, with a rope rigged through the bolt as a brake, began to carry me down the slabs at the belay to the steep sandy slope about 50 yards below. This involved much slipping, cursing, and tipping of the litter, which I found painful and alarming, and at one point a loose rock rolled down and crunched into the top of the litter and my helmet, which I was glad I had kept on. They finally found a spot where they could brace the foot of the litter against some rocks, reducing the angle at which I lay.

(The decision was made not to pick Paul up until the following morning, as his injuries were not severe and the park's contract helicopter was not available.)

In the morning, Mike made me a hot chicken stew, which I slurped with relish, and then the radio came to life. More members of the search and rescue team showed up, and they began to prepare me to be helicoptered out. While I had my misgivings about this, I realized there was really no other choice. When I mentioned my concerns to Keith, he said that the Braille Book incident had involved a military helicopter and reassured me that the park's contract helicopter pilot was excellent, and that I had nothing to worry about. Shortly thereafter we heard the distant "whop" of rotors, and I saw the helicopter fly up the valley. This was an image I had seen several times before, always wondering what had happened to some poor bastard. Now it was coming to get me—something I had never considered a possibility. As the helicopter approached El Cap, the pilot's voice came over the radio, perfectly calm and very precise, announcing his arrival. His voice gave me an immense sense of relief. The helicopter swept up to us, hovered a moment while the pilot examined the site, and then descended to El Cap meadow to wait for the team to get me ready to move.

The team then prepared me for the lift, securing my neck and head with a plastic collar, strapping me in the litter with webbing, and attaching the lift webbing to the frame of the litter. They then began to carry me another 50 yards to an open area away from the trees. This last carry, with my head downhill and the team again slipping and cursing, erased any final doubts I had about the necessity of the helicopter extraction.

The team put a sleeping bag over me to keep me warm in the cold downdraft of the rotors. They then called the helicopter, which I could hear approaching. When it got close, a team member put a shirt over my face to protect me from the sticks and dirt swept up by the downdraft. I heard them secure the webbing to the line from the helicopter and then felt the litter lift off the ground. As I began to rise, somebody took off the shirt, and I looked up and saw that I was suspended from a single 3/4-inch nylon rope hanging from the bottom of the helicopter. The co-pilot was looking down at me and talking into his helmet microphone to the pilot. Then the helicopter rose up slowly and I began to spin slightly. I could see El Cap, Sentinel, and the Cathedrals swirling by out of my peripheral vision. It occurred to me that it was probably just as well that I could not see down, or even out to the side very much. With infinite care, the pilot began to move off laterally and then to drop slightly. I realized he was taking care to minimize the amount of swing and even the amount of spin I experienced, although I did start to spin quit a bit. In a few minutes I could see trees in my peripheral vision and knew we were close to landing in El Cap meadows. A moment later, I heard voices and felt hands on the litter, and then my vision was filled with a ring of heads in firemen's helmets. At that moment, I felt a tremendous sense of release and was briefly overcome with emotion, fighting back a gush of hot tears that I didn't want the firefighters to see. I heard them unclip the line to the helicopter, and then they began loading me into the fire truck/ambulance. I was particularly touched by the kind manner of one woman firefighter, who seemed to be the crew boss, and who took particular care to speak to me as I was being loaded in the ambulance. She also rode with me to the clinic.

I felt the truck move off and trundle around the valley, eventually arriving at the Yosemite clinic. There the medical staff swarmed over me, taking off my harness and helmet, and getting me ready for x-rays. The clinic's doctor told me that they were concerned that I may have punctured a lung, and that they had seen what might have been an air pocket under the skin on my neck. As a consequence, he explained, they did not think it wise to send me to the hospital in Modesto by ambulance and had instead ordered a medical helicopter to fly me there. After the x-rays had been examined, I was put back in the ambulance and driven out to Ahwahnee Meadow, where a second helicopter was waiting. The EMT for the helicopter, a heavy-set older man, explained to me that during the flight, he would sit over me with a needle in his hand. If at any time it appeared that my lung was punctured and leaking air into my abdominal cavity, he would plunge the needle into my chest to let the air out and reinflate my lung. He said that it would be very painful. Fortunately, this wasn't necessary.

The second flight lasted about twenty minutes. I was wheeled out of the helicopter into an emergency room swarming with medical specialists of all types, wearing shower caps and baggies on their feet, who looked at me with extremely keen interest and anticipation. When my injuries were explained to them, most began to drift away in little groups. Two doctors came up to me and explained that they would need further x-rays and a CAT scan of my hip, which were taken with great efficiency. The orthopedist explained that I had a hairline fracture around the base of the ball at the head of the femur, and that he would reinforce this with three stainless steel screws. This operation occurred the next day while I was under general anesthesia. I spent the remainder of the week in the hospital. At the end of the week, friends brought me and my car home, and I began the process of learning for the second time in my life how to walk on crutches. Now, three weeks after the fall, I am just beginning to get around a bit without the crutches. The many scrapes have almost completely healed, and the huge purple welt over my right kidney has shrunk to a fraction its original size. I still have to sleep sitting up, but I have gotten used to that. Doctors say the ribs will heal in another three months or so, and that I should be able to start skiing in February. I expect to be back on the rock in the spring.

Analysis

In the last few years, I have become increasingly interested in first ascents and exploratory climbs of moderate difficulty. One consistent feature of this type of climbing is the presence of loose rock. While I have always had a tremendous respect for its dangers, and have had a few close brushes with rocks that others have knocked down on me or I on others, I had never before experienced anything as dangerous or as terrifying as the collapse of the big block I stepped on here. It was about half the size of a refrigerator, and seeing this rotate out from under my foot was horrifying. The block, and the cascade of smaller rocks its fall released, left a swath of destruction in the manzanita below and a pox of white impact scars on the ledges around the belay. Club members climbing on the other side of the valley heard the block crash down the slope. It could easily have killed me and both my partners, although Christian took shelter in a safe location after I suggested he do so. I had tapped the rock and thought it looked and sounded solid. I also thought it was big enough that my weight would not be enough to shift it. Obviously, I was wrong on both counts. If I continue climbing these exploratory types of routes, I will need to take an even more cautious approach to the dangers of loose rock, particularly the danger to the lower belayer. I will also be more likely to clip my double ropes separately, so that falling rock is less likely to sever them both at a single point, as nearly happened here.

The big question is, how could I have fallen 100 feet or more? I have been climbing traditional routes for almost 20 years, I carry a rack with double sets of stoppers and cams, I'm 56 and have the caution of those no longer young, and I know how to place gear. Unfortunately, I simply don't recall my gear placements on the climb, and no one has been back to the upper part of the climb to examine it (although Christian did go back and retrieve gear and ropes from the lower part of the climb). So I do not have a good analysis of why I fell so far. Christian was belaying me, and he said that he never let go of the rope, and in fact barely felt anything when the rope finally caught me, which is not surprising, given the amount of rope out when I fell.

I do have some ideas, however. I was climbing in chimneys that offered few gear placements and that were linked by easy ledges where I felt little need to place gear, so I did not have many pieces in. I had also picked up some rope drag about mid-rope and wanted to avoid putting in gear that would make the rope drag worse. I recall one placement that consisted merely of a sling girth hitched to a manzanita bush, the main purpose of which was to keep the rope running smoothly, away from a notched chockstone where the rope would otherwise have gotten stuck. I also girth- hitched an old but solid-looking oak stump about six inches thick. This stump, with my webbing still wrapped around it, ended up at the belay. I suspect the falling block smashed into it and ripped it out, since the top of it was broken, and the carabiner on the sling around the stump had a rough gouge in it.

And then there is the destroyed carabiner. One possibility is that this carabiner was attached to my highest piece, which is still in place, and that the block hit this as it fell. This might explain the gouges in the carabiner and in the sheaths of both of my 9mm Edelweiss Stratos ropes, which I had clipped together through my protection. The twisted, open, and dead gate may have been caused by the rope cross-loading the gate as I fell.

I also wonder if the block did not hit the first piece and snag the rope, jerking me out of the jam crack and into the air and clear of the rock like a trout yanked out of a stream. The sudden acceleration this would cause might explain why I have no memory of the start of the fall and why I did not fall into the chimney into which the rest of the loose rock was cascading. It might also explain the shredded back of my right hand, which was in a jam crack, and my wrenched right shoulder. Unfortunately, since my belayers were busy taking cover, and I was momentarily indisposed, no one will ever know how my fall path somehow kept me out of the chimneys and off the ledges I had climbed up.

I have also reflected on the injuries I received—and the ones I did not. My helmet had two small sharp gouges in it that could have been severe cuts if I had not been wearing it. The five broken ribs, the huge purple bruise over my right kidney, and the arching scrape mark on my back are almost certainly the result of my falling on the huge #5 and #6 Camalots I was carrying on the back of my harness for use in the chimneys. I am not sure how I could have avoided carrying them this way, but rest assured I will be thinking about it the next time I have occasion to carry them. Both my ankles were shredded because I was wearing low-cut shoes, and the right shoe was ripped off altogether in the fall. I wear low-cuts not by preference, but because it is almost impossible to find a decent pair of high top climbing shoes, the few available inevitably being low-end shoes designed for beginners. When are those bastards going to make a decent high-top? My right shin was severely barked due to the open, straight leg cotton pants I was wearing, which pulled up during the fall. If I had been wearing technical climbing pants with a tight zippered calf, as I do in cooler weather, I would probably still have the skin on my shins. The back of my right hand, which had been in a jam crack when I fell, was shredded and bleeding. Taping for the climb would have solved that problem.

One piece of gear I often worry about being injured by is my large Leeper cleaning tool. I used to carry this on a lightweight 'biner on my harness, with a cord for extension when in use. I became concerned, however, that this arrangement was too rigid, and could result in the tool puncturing my abdomen in a fall. Now I carry this on my harness hanging from a long enough piece of cord that it can move around freely in a fall. It caused no problems in this fall, although one end of the gear loop it was clipped into ripped out of the harness.

When I stopped falling, one of the two ropes was wrapped around my thigh, squeezing it painfully. Fortunately, Christian was able to cut the rope at the harness, releasing the pressure. If I had been hanging alone on a wall, well above the belay, this problem might not have been worked out so easily. I carry a tiny knife on my harness for cutting old webbing out of bolts, and I could have used this, but I was in so much pain and had so much trouble moving that it might have taken a long time to do the job, and if I was on a vertical wall, I would have needed to stay tied in anyway. I can only say that the outcome of this one was mighty lucky.

I also wondered if I wasn't lucky to have fallen all the way to the belay. If I had taken a shorter fall, but with the same injuries, my partners would have had to climb up to me and try to get me down. Just the climbing up part could have been problematic. As I climbed the second chimney, I realized that my partners would probably find it very difficult to follow, even with a tight top-rope. If I had been injured and helpless above this chimney, particularly with worse injuries than I had, the experience could have become a very long and very unpleasant ordeal. While I only climb at a moderate level myself, it is not unusual for me to climb with partners who have difficulty following what I lead, and who would be hard pressed to get up to me if I were injured without a very well managed tight line. This has also been a sobering realization.

I was glad to have two partners, and this was not an accident. Increasingly, I climb in groups of three or four, in part because I enjoy the socializing, in part because I appreciate the greater security of larger parties, particularly for more remote, exploratory climbs. I routinely climb with two 9mm Edelweiss Stratos ropes, using the Petzl Reverso, a self-locking belay device that allows a leader to safely belay two followers simultaneously on two ropes. Using the Reverso allows a party of three to climb almost as fast as a party of two, at least on moderate terrain.

I like to believe that accidents aren't really accidental, and I believe that is true here. Some part of me didn't want to climb that weekend, and when I didn't listen, it found a way to get my attention. I was tired from a long week of work, and I wanted to stay home, rest up, work on the house, and socialize in town. I was also coming to believe that exploring the possibility of a new relationship might be a lot more of an adventure than exploring another rock climbing route. But I had made a commitment to my partners to go, and although I knew they wouldn't really mind if I didn't, I felt I had given my word and was duty-bound to carry through. And when we got up on the Lost Brother, some part of me was not really enthusiastic about exploring those ugly-looking chimneys. It was an idea we had, but I felt little joy at the prospect as I led out. In short, I wasn't psyched to climb, and that is a vulnerable state to be in when leading.

In the end, I paid a price for not honoring my own spirit. The consequences were harsh, but far less so than they could have been. I consider myself the luckiest unlucky guy in the world. (Source: Paul Minault)
(*Editor's Note: Paul Minault's analysis covers a lot of ground, and as a result, fewer narratives on California are included this year. We thank Paul, one of the pioneers for The Access Fund, for his contribution.*)

FALL ON ROCK, INADEQUATE PROTECTION, INADEQUATE CLOTHING AND EQUIPMENT, WEATHER
California, Yosemite Valley, El Capitan

At 4 a.m. on September 30, I (Tom Randall—22) started up Eagle's Way, VI 5.8 A3, on El Cap, in an attempt to break the solo record. I had checked the weather with the rangers at the Wilderness Center and was given, "...sunny for the next two days," (ample time for me to do the route) and received the same from a telephone weather line two hours before I started.

I climbed straight through the day and was cleaning pitch 11 after dark that evening when my headlamp battery ran out. I had a brand new spare with me, which turned out to be a total dud and gave out after half an hour on pitch 12. No big problem. I just lowered off to the belay and settled down for a night in my comfy harness—but it did put me ten hours behind.

The next morning, I finished leading pitch 12 and got all racked up for 13. I was belaying with a Grigri connected to the belay loop on my seat harness by a brand new DMM Belay Master locking carabiner. To back up the Grigri I periodically tied a knot in the free side of the rope and clipped it to my harness, leaving several feet of slack between the knot and the Grigri so that I could do a few moves.

The pitch went bolt (which I back-cleaned), rivet (to which I attached a big, beefy, hanger), copperhead (back-cleaned), RURP (back-cleaned), RURP (back-cleaned), copperhead. I was on the copperhead and had just taken my adjustable daisy from the RURP and was reaching up to the next placement when, "PING!" the copperhead pulled.

I fell 20 feet back to the rivet, the hanger broke, and I continued directly onto the belay—factor 2! The rope came tight on my Grigri, but then the locking carabiner just snapped off and I continued to fall for another 20 feet, which was the slack to my backup knot—all that kept me from the talus field below. When I came to a stop, the Grigri was 20 feet above me still on the rope. The total fall was about 60 feet.

On the way down I flipped upside down and took some pretty bad rope burns to my left hand (I'm left handed). I could hardly use the hand and the fall had inflamed an old back injury.

I ascended to the belay and weighed my options. I badly wanted to do this route in a good time. How fast could I lead, clean and jug each pitch now? It had taken me 20 minutes to jug 40 feet to the anchor. Also my Grigri is mangled—a screw sheared off and the plastic piece pushed out by the loss of the 'biner—so I'm going to have use a slower system. I can stand up straight, but bending over or exerting my back muscles in any way is killing me. To cut a long story short—I asked for a rescue. Yes, I hated myself for it and I know that it was the wimp's way out. But at least I'm a wimp who gets to live another day.

The rescue went fine, despite the fact that the "sunny" forecast had turned into a stormy afternoon, with rain and snow showers. The rescuer was lowered from the top, as vertically, I think I was only a few hundred feet below the rim. We then lowered together on 1200-foot-long ropes tied together to reach the ground.

Analysis

The Belay Master is normally equipped with a plastic guard that prevents cross-loading the 'biner, by separating the harness and the Grigri. But the guard on mine had been stolen so I had decided to go without one. We never found the 'biner, but I think it most likely became cross-loaded between the Grigri and the harness loop, dropping it's breaking strength to well within the danger zone.

Does the Grigri itself create stopping forces that are dangerously high? Petzl does not approve it for this type of climbing, but a lot of us use it anyway.

Was I wrong to have back cleaned the bolt? It was my first—and only—solid piece and it would have decreased my fall factor. I thought about it, but the bolt was about six feet to the right and level with the belay, and the belay was built to take an upward pull. I could have put a long sling on the bolt, but straight above was a nice rivet. So I decided to take what I thought at the time was a small risk: I would keep the belay aligned by back-cleaning the bolt and clipping the rivet. That was the BIG error. I didn't think I was going to fall in the first easy 25 feet of climbing, and I didn't think that a big rivet hanger would break. And next time I'll take along some shock absorbers for those critical pieces.

ALWAYS tie a back-up knot!! I have always been one to say, "I won't happen to me!" or, "His gear only broke because it was probably 15 years old and he kept it in a bucket of acid..." But now we know—these things do happen to me and it could be anyone. I can't really express how glad I am that I took the precaution.

I don't remember who said that about the combination of errors and bad luck that leads to failure situations, but I couldn't agree more. Think of all those days out when one little thing happens and it leads to nothing and you think, "Oh, that was lucky." Well one day, all those little things may happen at once. (Source: Tom Randall)

NPS Comments

Tom made several mistakes in his selection and use of climbing gear. Our main issue, however, is not his choice of belay or protection technique, but his preparation for surviving on El Cap in case he were stranded in bad weather—as happened in this case. Like most speed climbers, he took only a lightweight set of clothing—a couple of warm undershirts, a fleece top, a storm jacket, a hat, and gloves—but no other storm gear or shelter. This was completely insufficient for sitting out a storm. Furthermore, he had only one rope for retreat and less than a day's worth of food—especially given all the calories required of a solo ascent. Finally, he took one used headlamp battery and only one spare—that failed.

The weather, in fact was cold, windy, and cloudy, with intermittent rain and snow squalls. Our concern wasn't Tom's injuries, which seemed stable (though painful), but hypothermia during the night to come, given his lack of gear. A large search was in progress in the high country, which tied up most of our resources. To get a team quickly to the top of El Cap we had to pull our helicopter and some team members off the search, and then hope for a safe flying window during breaks in the weather. We managed to fly between squalls, and decided to lower Tom all the way to the bottom of the route rather than raise him, because another flight—to get him off the top—was not guaranteed. After the rescue, the team rappelled the East Ledges descent route.

Tom based his decision to start the route on the weather forecast, which he checked from two different sources, but both sources use the same original information. Every experienced climber should know that you should not rely upon the weather forecast in the mountains.

Tom is right about the compounding effect of a series of errors and bad luck. How many of each can you find in this account? For more on this accident see "British Soloist Charged with Reckless Endangerment" in the aid climbing forum on www.rockclimbing.com. (Source: John Dill—Park Ranger, Yosemite National Park)

FAILED TO TURN BACK, INADEQUATE CLOTHING AND EQUIPMENT, WEATHER, POOR POSITION—BIVOUAC SITE
California, Split Mountain

In October, the climb up our twelfth 14,000-foot peak, Split Mountain, did not go well. One member of our climbing party, Dave French, was hospitalized for frostbite afterward and is still recovering.

It was early October. Dave, his son Sean, Sean's friend Matt, their college professor Tom Campbell and I were expecting late summer conditions with fair weather and little wind. We did not realize however, that a storm earlier in the week had left seven to ten inches of snow above 9,000 feet, or that cold temperatures since then had left the snow as a dry powder. We were surprised to see the snow on the mountains when we arrived but we felt that it would probably burn off before we reached it and that any remaining would not be a significant factor anyway.

The first day we hiked from a low start on the valley floor, up Red Creek to Red Lake. We camped there with nine other climbers in three groups all headed for Split Mountain the next morning. It seemed odd that such a pristine area would be hosting so many climbers that late in the season. We suspected this out-of-the-way eastern Sierra trail had been largely ignored before the recent interest in California's fourteener's.

We were first out of camp at 6:30 the next morning with the other climbers close behind. At head of the Red Creek Canyon is a glacial cirque, which in normal conditions would have been an easy Class 3 climb up a steep chute of loose scree. The layer of dry snow meant that we were still walking on loose scree, but we couldn't see it. Add to this the fact that in many sections, between large rocks and in the bottom of the chute for example, the snow had drifted to waist depth and beyond, and you have very difficult climbing conditions.

It was slow going, especially the last hundred feet, which was particularly steep. Tom and I were first up. By the time Dave, Sean and finally Matt had mounted the cirque and turned toward the peak it was after noon. One of the other climbing parties, a man and his two sons, had passed us and started up the peak about 15 minutes before. The six climbers behind us had given up and turned back short of the top of the cirque.

From the top of the cirque at 13,000 feet, the summit climb looked easy, but it was not. The north side of the peak is less steep than the cirque, but the climbing conditions were just as bad with a dry powder over talus and scree. There was no crust on the snow. It could not support a climber's weight. Each step was supported by the surface below, which often did not provide a good footing, especially with a layer of compressed powder under your boot. Often your boot would fall between unseen rocks. Occasionally we crossed drifts where we sunk in above our waists.

I did not have sunglasses and was concerned about snow blindness. As we started toward the summit I covered my prescription glasses with strips of adhesive tape from the medical kit I was carrying. I left a narrow gap between the strips and used my fingernail to open additional slits. I alternated between eyes while climbing and closed them both during rests.

Even beyond the difficult conditions, our progress was very slow. Tom was in the lead. Dave and Sean were stopping for rests often and waiting for Matt to catch up. I had dropped back when I taped over my glasses and after catching up had stayed back with Matt to encourage him.

A couple hundred feet above the cirque Tom turned around and walked back down to the rest of the group. He said that the last hundred feet had taken us 30 minutes and there was not time to make it to the peak and back down before dark. He said he was not prepared to bivouac and so was heading back. Sean and Matt were willing to turn around too.

I was not. It was still early afternoon. I didn't think we needed to make it back to camp before dark; we just needed to get off the top of the cirque. We had a couple headlamps with us and could walk the rest of the way after dark.

Dave also wanted to go on. He didn't want to have to come back up Split Mountain before finishing the fourteeners. (He and I had just four more peaks left.) He said that we had enough equipment with us and should be able to bivouac if we had to. Tom and Matt turned back. Dave, Sean (who decided to stay with his father), and I went on. Before separating Dave asked Matt to leave me with his bivy sack and headlamp.

A while later we passed the two boys coming down. They had not made the peak and had decided to turn around. They were going to wait for their father at the top of the chute. About an hour later their father also passed us. He had made the summit. The climb to the peak was very slow with frequent stops for rest. We took some pictures and started back down at 4:30 p.m., two hours before sunset.

On the way down, the wind came up. Waiting for Dave and Sean I started to feel cold, and with that a bit of apprehension. We were at high altitude late in the day and late in the season. Hoping to speed things up I commented that we could not spend the night here. We had not yet resigned ourselves to a bivouac but realized that if we were going on we had to find the chute we came up and get down the steepest part before dark. Without ropes there was no other reasonable route and the top portion was simply too difficult to downclimb after dark.

I thought the chute was at the low point in the pass to our north. Sean said it was to the northeast. I decided to go ahead of Dave and Sean to make sure we located it before dark. I went toward the northeast first to pick up our outbound tracks. I found a very light track in the snow with clear switchbacks and followed it north. I assumed that the rest of our tracks were running parallel to this further to the east or had been covered by the blowing snow. Sean became alarmed when he saw me continuing further down the ridge to the north. He yelled after me that I had gone too far. He checked his altimeter and yelled that the pass was only 70 feet below him. Dave yelled after him that it was 170 feet below. Sean corrected him, but I didn't get this message and thought that 170 feet was more consistent with where I thought the pass was. Sean was sure that this was wrong and stopped to get a GPS reading before continuing down. He had both his GPS and his altimeter watch with him. Further, he had checked the altitude and stored a fix at the top of the chute.

With Dave and Sean now stopped on the slope above me, I took my headlamp out of my fanny pack and left the pack with the second headlamp out in the open where they could see it. My idea was that if I could locate the chute I could mark it with my light and guide them to it. I went toward the edge of the ridge to my east to see what was below. In the waning light I could see that the canyon below was not the canyon we had come up, but rather a canyon further north. To the south I could just make out an arête, which I recognized as being on the north side of the cirque we had come up.

By this time Sean had a GPS reading and he and Dave had started back up the ridge toward the southeast. I picked up the pack and hurried back up the ridge to join them. By the time we were back together it was dark and continuing to look for the chute, even with the GPS and headlamps seemed pointless. We could not climb down in the dark.

We decided to bivouac. We started to move away from the pass to avoid the wind but then decided to just dig into the snow where we were instead. The snow was only about a foot deep at that spot. We cleared a four by six foot patch, stacking the snow from the clearing on the windward side. We then got out our bivy bags. None of us had used or even seen this equipment before. It was still in its original packaging.

I had thought that each of us had a bivy bag, but it turns out we only had two, the one Matt had left me and an identical one Sean carried. Dave was carrying a space blanket instead. Dave thought that we would be able to double up in one of the bags for warmth and use the space blanket as added insulation. But the bivy bags were not big enough for two of us to get into.

The space blanket was not long enough to extend all the way to Dave's feet and still cover his shoulders. Further it was not wide enough to completely wrap around him so he just tucked the sides in under him. The wind kept pulling the sides out. The Mylar was flapping in the wind most of the night. I got up to help tuck in his legs a couple of times. The last time the Mylar had ripped so I just took what was left and wrapped it around his legs a couple of times.

During the night Dave expressed a concern about getting frostbite on his toes. I didn't know and didn't answer the question directly. Instead I suggested that we alternately curl and straighten our toes every few minutes to keep the blood flowing. Dave relayed this message to Sean who was on the other side of him. About 2:30 in the morning, Dave could no longer wiggle his toes.

At some point I suggested that Dave and Sean breathe into their jackets to preserve body heat. It was a long night. My fingers and toes were numb and I was at times shivering more violently than I have ever before. Despite the cold I fell asleep several times.

We waited for the sun before getting up the next morning, found the chute easily and headed back toward camp. At that point we didn't know that anything was wrong. Tom and Matt had come up the trail looking for us and met us half way down.

We were back in camp before noon. Dave took his boots off to rest before we walked on down to the car. His toes were heavily blistered and discolored. The blisters were orange and were not located at wear points as hiking blisters usual are. And the ends of several toes were black.

Dave ended up hospitalized for a week and continued Jacuzzi treatments and medication for one month. Although he did not lose any of his toes, he still has not fully regained feeling in them. Although not discolored or blistered, my toes and fingertips tingled for about three weeks after the climb. I assume this is the result of some pre-frostbite condition.

Analysis

We made an astounding collection of errors. The most obvious of course is the failure to turn back when the climb proved more difficult than we had planned for. But to end the discussion here would be a great oversimplification. We went on expecting to hike back after dark and we had accepted the possibility of a bivouac if we couldn't. We've hiked through the night before and we've bivouacked successfully before, and we should have been able to in this case.

I did not bring sufficient clothing. I had made a religion out of traveling light, taking only that which I was sure to use. This left little margin for the unexpected. My predicament hit home while I was waiting for Dave and Sean near the peak. The only way I had kept warm during the climb was by moving. A few minutes without moving and I was cold. This is absurd. You should be able to stop anytime for as long as needed; whether for a broken leg, a tired partner or, as in this case, wet gloves.

We were not familiar with the emergency equipment we were carrying. If we had examined this equipment before the climb, we would have been much less receptive to the idea of a bivouac!

We underestimated the effect of the first new snow of the season. We have hiked across plenty of snowfields and glaciers, but this was different. The dry powder with no solid layer underneath it was really difficult to move across. None of us had gaiters to keep the snow out of our boots and I didn't even have sunglasses; but the real problem was how much the snow slowed us down.

My getting lost on the way back to the top of the chute cost us the opportunity to walk out that night. This is particularly disconcerting considering we had the technology available to prevent us from ever getting lost. That I forgot about the GPS and that I was not paying enough attention on the way up to recognize my surroundings on the way back is mortifying. But a deeper concern is my willingness, like every lost hiker ever, to adjust reality to fit my perception of it. I was sure we had come up from the lower pass. And I don't know who made the single track I followed down to it, but it was certainly not the trail of eight people going up and five going back down within the last six hours. The real trail was further east and it was not covered by the blowing snow. In fact it was still quite visible the next morning!

The location of our bivouac, right at the top of the pass, was poor. It's virtually always windy at the top of a pass. This night was no exception. Of course, it would have been difficult to get away from the wind. Along the same lines, we needed to dig in deeper. The shallow hole we dug in the thin snow near the pass did not keep the wind off of us and the snow berm we formed on the upwind side was completely ineffective. In fact, the berm was probably triggering turbulent flow downstream! We would have been better off in the laminar boundary layer flow without the berm. We also would have been better off if we had taken the extra snow and covered ourselves with it. Snow is an excellent insulator and on this night there would have been little concern for it melting.

We would have been much better off if we had gone back to one of the deep snowdrifts we had passed through and dug snow caves. My experience with snow caves has been that they are comfortable and completely insulated from the wind.

One simple trick to keeping your feet warm is to loosen up your boots. This allows more blood to flow through the less constricted veins. I've always known this. In fact, I even thought of it on the way up. Sean's boots laces had come loose and I was helping him lace them back up. The laces were frozen. I had to suck on them to get them untied. Then when I pulled them tight, the laces broke. There wasn't enough length left to make a bow so I had just knotted what remained. That's when I thought about loosening them at night and realized how hard this would be now that they were knotted. Still, Dave and I could have easily loosened our boots, and Sean's other boot could have been loosened. But I didn't think of it again once we had bivouacked for the night. And despite our numb feet, we never unlaced our boots!

My climbing gloves were of no use. The material between the fingers, which end just at the first knuckles, holds the bare fingers apart. This makes them excellent heat radiators! I believe my hands would have been warmer if I had closed my fists without gloves. I the future I'll bring either full gloves or mittens.

We had adhesive tape in our medical kit. We could have taped Dave's space blanket on him. This would have been much better than leaving it to flap in the wind and eventually tear. I could also have used the tape to keep the top of my bag closed, or to cover the vent if I had known it was there. More significantly, we could have slit the sewn seams on mating sides of the two bivy bags, then used the tape to fasten them together as one big bag that we all could have fit inside. We would have been much warmer with three of us on the inside and Dave would have been out of the wind. And if we had taped the space blanket inside the top of this double bag, so it reflected our body heat, I suspect we would have been downright comfortable!

Why did we not think of these "solutions" on the mountain? Certainly we had time to cogitate on our predicament as we lay awake that night. Dave and I theorized that perhaps the lack of oxygen at altitude or the cold temperatures compromised our reasoning ability. If so, it's all the more important that we review and analyze the experience after the fact. We need to decide in advance what were going to do differently next time if we can't trust the decisions we make while climbing.

Another theory is that we may not have been looking for "solutions." As climbers we have a fairly high capacity for pain and a tendency to put up with whatever is thrown at us. At one point during the night Dave asked Sean what time it was. We didn't know if we had been laying there for two hours or twelve. When Sean answered that it was two in the morning, we were all relieved. We had already made it through eight hours. Just four more and this would all be over. I think that same mentality—"let's just tough this out"—may have taken over hours before; perhaps even while we were still climbing up toward the peak.

We were fortunate. If the temperature had been ten degrees colder the outcome would have been much more serious. Not all our decisions were poor. The arrangement with the three of us laying on our sides and pressed together worked well for all of us and provided some protection for Dave, who without a bivy bag was at least in the middle. However, he is considerably taller than either Sean or me. This left his feet out in the cold.

It was also good that we did not attempt to climb down the chute after dark. There was no discussion or argument on this point, we just turned away. That's encouraging. On this matter there would have been little room for misjudgment. (Source: Mike Koerner)

(Editor's Note: Another lengthy narrative, but filled with illustrative lessons from the best source: the individual involved.)

EXPOSURE—WEATHER, INADEQUATE CLOTHING AND EQUIPMENT, HYPOTHERMIA, FALL ON ROCK—UNABLE TO COMPLETE DESCENT
California, Yosemite Valley, El Capitan

In late December, Joseph Crowe (25) began fixing pitches on the Zodiac (VI 5.7, A) on El Capitan, intending to solo the route. By mid-afternoon on the 5th, he was just finishing pitch-3 with plans to fix pitch-4 and to return to the ground that evening.

Two other climbers, Pat Warren and Matt Robertson, had camped at the base of the route near Crowe the previous night. When they started hiking down to the road in late afternoon on the 5th, Crowe appeared to be leading pitch-4. Although the weather that morning had been mostly cloudy and windy, with scattered light rain and a temperature of about 40 degrees F, they noticed that Crowe had dressed in fairly light clothing and did not appear to have taken any extra storm clothing up the wall with him. The first few pitches of the route were known to be particularly exposed and they had previously seen Crowe return from fixing pitches, thoroughly soaked by water coming off the summit and blown in by the wind.

A short time later a storm moved in, with high wind, heavy rain and snow. Visibility quickly deteriorated to 20-30 feet. Warren and Robertson were not too concerned about Crowe since he had the skills and enough rope to get down, and the three climbers had talked together in camp about rapping off a route if severe weather struck. But as they were hiking past the Nose about 6:30 p.m, after dark, they heard cries for help coming from the vicinity of the Zodiac and they were sure it was Crowe. They themselves had become soaked by the storm during the hike, despite good foul weather gear and they were now very concerned for Crowe.

At 7:30 p.m. they reported the situation to the NPS. Using a loudspeaker from the road, the rangers got answering cries, but the storm made communications extremely difficult. They did manage to determine that he was still on the wall, had no light, and was unable to get down. SAR team members hiked to the base of the route (which took almost two hours because of the conditions). When they arrived, they found Crowe hanging from etriers attached to the end of a rope, 25-30 feet off the ground and 15 feet out from the wall. He was not moving and did not answer their calls. After more gear was brought to the scene, they were able to fix a line to him by means of a carabiner attached to a long pole. A ranger ascended a fixed line (left earlier by other climbers) on Shortest Straw (an adjacent route), carrying the line that was fixed to Crowe. He pulled the two of them together and lowered Crowe to the ground. Despite attempts to revive Crowe, he was pronounced dead from hypothermia by a physician at the Yosemite clinic.

Analysis

A few days after the accident, NPS team members climbed the first four pitches of the Zodiac and analyzed Crowe's rigging. Based on that evidence, here is the most likely series of events:

Crowe was climbing with two dynamic ropes, one 70 meters (230 feet) long and the other 55 meters (180 feet). He had previously fixed them from the ground to pitch-3, and on this day he pulled them up to climb pitch-4. When he finished the pitch, or if he needed to descend earlier, he would rely on those ropes to return to the base of the wall, as their combined lengths were more than adequate to do so from the top of pitch-4.

The 70 meter rope was his lead rope. It was tied to the anchor at the top of pitch-3 (the "pitch-3 anchor"), but instead of the end of the rope being tied there, the knot was about 15 feet from the end, leaving a tail of that length hanging down pitch-3. His belay device was probably his Grigri.

For some reason, possibly the storm, darkness, or a technical problem, Crowe stopped climbing about 20 feet short of the regular pitch-4 anchor and built his own anchor out of protection he placed in the crack. Then, using his Grigri, he rappelled on the free part of the 70 meter rope, leaving the part on which he had led still clipped through the protection and anchored at pitch-3. He did not clean the pitch as he descended, possibly because he was in a hurry and also because he wanted to eventually return and complete the pitch. By leaving a significant amount of the 70 meter rope tied up in the pitch, he was relying on the remaining free part plus the 55 meter rope to reach the ground.

Crowe rappelled to the pitch-3 anchor. At this point he was still rappelling on the free part of the 70 meter rope. About 40 feet below him, a knot joined the end of this rope to one end of the 55 meter rope. The other end of the 55 meter rope was tied to the 15-foot tail of the 70 meter rope that hung from the pitch-3 anchor. As a result, the 55 meter rope hung from both the free side (on which he was rappelling) and the anchor side of the 70 meter rope, forming a continuous loop. This was apparently a solo aid technique he was trying.

The bottom of the loop was about 100 feet below him, well above the ground. To gain the full length of the 55 meter rope, he would have to descend about 15 feet past the level of the pitch-3 anchor, reach over and untie the joining knot in the anchor side of the loop, and drop that end of the 55 meter rope. Then he would rappel another 25 feet, pass the remaining joining knot, and continue descending on the 55 meter rope, hopefully to the base of the wall.

It may have been dark by now, certainly windy and cold, with almost no visibility, and he may have been in the waterfall that targets pitch-3. With his minimal clothing he was probably hypothermic, in a hurry, and possibly panicked. His light, a very small LED model (found later in his pocket), would have been useless, and he may have had to determine the dimensions of his system and the location of the critical anchor-side knot by memory and feel, with numb fingers.

Either he had forgotten that both ends of the 55 meter rope were tied into the system, or he misjudged the distance to the anchor-side knot, for he descended past the level of the knot. In fact he continued at least another 25 feet until he had passed the knot on his side of the loop and was now on the 55 meter rope. At some point he realized that he had gone too far and would have to ascend to reach the anchor-side knot.

As he climbed back up the 55 meter rope, he accidentally jammed his upper ascender tightly up against the knot he had just passed. He was unable to free the ascender, and since it was tied with cord, rather than clipped, to his harness, he cut it loose. (After the accident the ascender was found jammed against the free-side knot.)

With only one ascender, Crowe was unable or unwilling to continue up the rope (although it was feasible with the remaining ascender and a prusik). He apparently decided to go with what rope he could get at that point. He reached over to the anchor side of the loop and cut the 55 meter rope, opening the loop. (We found the 55 meter rope on the anchor side of the loop cut at the level of the jammed ascender.) This left 25 feet of the 55 meter rope hanging uselessly below the anchor-side knot, shortening the rope available to reach the ground by that amount.

Then he tied a safety knot in the end he had cut, dropped that end, and—leaving two etriers behind with the abandoned ascender—rappelled about 150 feet until he reached the end of the rope. He was now 30 feet above the ground and 15 feet away from the wall. With his tiny light, in a whiteout, we wonder if he knew how close he was.

His subsequent actions may have been accomplished in a different order, but here's one reasonable sequence: Hanging just above the end of the

55-meter rope, he attached his remaining ascender to the rope just above his Grigri. He clipped his two remaining etriers in series to the ascender, making a long ladder. He stepped onto the ladder and cut the 55-meter rope between the ascender and the Grigri. (We found a two-foot piece of the 55-meter rope, cut at both ends, with the Grigri attached and what was probably the safety knot still tied. We don't know why he didn't just unclip the Grigri, but we suspect his fingers were too cold by then.)

He then cut the cord connecting his harness to his ascender and began to climb down the ladder, unbelayed. If he had reached the bottom step and hung from his hands he would have faced a drop of only 15 feet. If he had not abandoned the other two etriers, he could have almost stepped onto the ground. But he probably collapsed from hypothermia and fell, and his hammer became entangled in the etriers. He was found suspended by the shoulder sling of the hammer, with no evidence that he had tried to cut himself free.

The lack of adequate storm clothing and a headlamp with useful range were his most serious problems With that gear he probably could have stayed on the wall through the storm or descended with more control. As it was, if he had searched carefully for the anchor-side knot, if he had not jammed his ascender, if he had been able to fashion a prusik, and if he had found and untied the knot, he would have gained 25 feet more of the 55 meter rope, enough to reach his goal. (Sources: Jack Hoeflich and John Dill—Park Rangers, Yosemite National Park)

(Editor's Note: A correction from last year's ANAM, page 31: John Dill is quoted as saying, "...leads Grigri free to 5.10b..." and "...leads Grigri free 5.9, aid A2." It should read, "... leads trad free..." etc. Gremlins, not John Dill, caused this typo.)

FALL ON ICE, INADEQUATE PROTECTION, EXCEEDING ABILITIES
Colorado, Ouray, Ouray Ice Park

John Ohlson (61) was leading Pic O' the Vic (WI 4) in the Ouray Ice Park. He led up to a stance at a cave—about 20 feet up, and placed an ice screw. He then continued up the next section, which was nearly vertical. About 20 feet above his screw placement, he came off. He essentially landed at the base of the climb. The rope did not come taut until the very end of his fall, and likely provided minor deceleration at most.

John sustained compression fractures to the T12 vertebra, a broken right thumb, and lacerations to his hands and face. Various others treated him at the scene. At first he thought he could walk out, but concern for the severity of his injuries prompted rescue personnel to raise him from the canyon bottom by winch on a litter with a body splint. He was taken by ambulance to Montrose Memorial Hospital.

Analysis

Ohlson had a long history of alpine climbs with modest technical difficulty, but he was a relatively new water ice climber. He had been training hard the previous week with this particular objective in mind. He had done a lot of top roped climbs of difficulties similar to this, all without incident or falls. His leads had not previously exceeded WI3+. He felt he was ready for this climb but still ran into difficulty. Clearly, the protection was inadequate, as it failed to keep him from grounding. He may not have been as well prepared as he felt he was. (Source: Steve Firebaugh—The Mountaineers)

A few comments additional comments by John Ohlson
A humbling experience, but I have fully recovered and now lead comparable ice nearly a year later. Time and more experience provide a useful perspective. I was not as well prepared as I thought. I attribute my fall directly to my inexperience with water ice variability, which requires substantial experience to judge reliably. This cannot be overemphasized to novice leaders on water ice, irrespective of their other climbing skills.

My ground-fall became possible by my running out the lead, raising a related issue. I am a conservative rock climber and place pro liberally. However, as others do, when the climbing is easy, I run it out to save time and energy, particularly for alpine climbing where speed is safety. Where I fell was easier than the vertical section I had just readily passed and I felt fully in control. My fall was a complete surprise. Since ice is more deceptive and less reliable than rock, running out a lead, particularly to the second screw, is a dangerous habit that long-time rock climbers must suppress, at the very least until they are experienced with ice quality.

FALL ON ROCK, MISCOMMUNICATION
Colorado, Rocky Mountain National Park, Lumpy Ridge, Whiteman

On March 20, there was a very nasty accident up at Lumpy Ridge that happened to a very experienced climber (in his 30's). He fell about 110 feet from the top anchor of the first pitch of Whiteman (11c, Guillotine Wall at Lumpy) due to apparent miscommunication between himself and his belayer on the ground.

He led the first pitch (Whiteman, 11c) successfully and arrived at the anchor (fixed slings, etc.). He thought he was going to be lowered. Meanwhile, the belayer was still on the ground and NOT tied in. He thought the leader was going to bring him up. So when the leader got to the anchors, he took him off belay. The leader leaned back ... and fell in a horizontal position. Upon nearing the ground, his upper body struck a tree, which rotated him into a vertical (feet first) position, which probably saved his life.

He suffered multiple broken bones and internals, but his skull and spine are intact. He's going to be ok in time. What a miracle.

Analysis
It's another one of these cases we've been hearing about lately—someone getting grievously hurt for lack of proper communication or attention to ordinary details.

During the examination of the scene, two camming (SLCD) devices placed on a "zig-zag" section of the pitch were found to have signs of been put under force/tension (inverted and "locked" in place). The friction of the rope running through this "zig-zag" may have helped to slow the acceleration of his fall. He may have also fallen through or hit the branches of a tree which is immediate to the base of the rock where he landed.

His partner does not usually carry a cell phone when climbing, and says that the phone was taken on this day as an after thought. During interviews with both climbers, they retrospectively acknowledged their mutual lack of maintaining clear communication and/or discussing choice of tactics to use. (Sources: William Alexander—Park Ranger, Rocky Mountain National Park, and Leo Paik)

FALL ON ROCK, CLIMBING ALONE, INADEQUATE PROTECTION, INADEQUATE EQUIPMENT—NO HELMET AND NO CLIMBING SHOES
Colorado, Eldorado State Park, Red Garden Wall

On September 14, Kirk Chynoweth (31) was soloing Redguard on Red Garden Wall when he fell about 50 feet. Two people got up to the victim before Alex and I did. Then the EMT and others members of Rocky Mountain Rescue jugged up immediately thereafter. He had cranial and wrist fractures and had to have his chest popped twice to relieve pleural pressure. We lowered him 120 feet to a ledge and then he was helicoptered to a hospital in Denver.

Analysis

There were a couple odd details with this one. The victim was rope soloing with a Grigri and gear. When he fell, he wasn't wearing his climbing shoes or a helmet. He also had a #4 Camalot with two lobes wired shut (probably because the trigger had broken). One of the two lobes that did function had a severely bent wire with a little fraying.

He landed on a sloping, rocky ledge that was maybe 50 feet up and right from the anchors of the first pitch of T2. One account from a member of RMR that happened to be climbing Touch and Go at the time of the accident said that the soloist probably fell from 20 feet above his anchor. His anchor had three pieces for upward pull (a small stopper, a medium stopper and a small/medium sized cam). He also had one larger cam clove hitched to the rope for downward pull. (Source: Leo Paik)

FALL ON ROCK, INADEQUATE EQUIPMENT—ROPE TOO SHORT, FAILURE TO TIE STOPPER KNOT, NO HARD HAT
Colorado, Eldorado Canyon, Red Garden Wall

On October 13, Kelly Elverum (34) was being lowered down Darkness 'til Dawn (5.9+) when the end of the climbing rope slipped through the belay device because the rope was not long enough to reach to the ground. The fall was about 35 feet, and the climber sustained serious head injuries. Neither climber was wearing a helmet.

Analysis

One way to prevent this from happening if one is not sure as to whether the rope will be long enough is to secure the end of the rope at the belay stance.

Leo Paik has this to say: As far as I know, there has never been an accident on Darkness 'til Dawn before. Myself, for Darkness, I usually take two ropes (which works well for protecting the traverse moves into the corner low down). The one-rope descent is to rappel/lower carefully to very close to the end of the rope, then scramble down 25 feet or so on steep third-class rock. (Sources: Steve Muelhauser—Park Manager II, Eldorado Canyon, and Leo Paik)

(Editor's Note: There were a total of eight accidents reported from Eldorado Canyon this year. Two of them seemed to be hikers or scramblers who got caught in a climbing situation. Four were the result of inadequate protection, and one involved pulling loose a rock that nearly severed a finger.)

FALL ON ROCK—UNCONTROLLED RAPPEL, INADEQUATE BACKUP
Colorado, Clear Creak Canyon

On October 20, I took a friend out to climb. It was her very first time, so I wanted to toprope something that was fairly easy. The climb is called Countersuit, a 5.9 toprope. She's very athletic so I thought a 5.9 would be a good challenge. The anchors (a set of bolts, each bolt with a chain) were on the vertical portion of the cliff; the ends of the chains were about two feet down the vertical cliff. The cliff edge was very prominent, I mean that the horizontal area above the cliff edge was very flat and the cliff edge was basically a 90-degree angle. The cliff-face directly over the edge was fairly featureless and about ten feet down became a little overhanging. I sat on the edge of the cliff and set up the toprope. I used quickdraws, one on each chain with the gates opposing. This made the point of rope anchorage to the cliff edge about 2.5 feet. I then setup a directional anchor down the cliff edge about 15 feet. When the toprope was set up, it was basically a big upside-down U. This would make it possible for us to toprope two climbs with the same rope.

I had my friend on the ground anchor one end of the rope so that I could rappel off a single rope. I rappelled off the anchors that I originally discussed. I would need to lower myself over the edge of the cliff and down about three feet before my belay device (an ATC) would become active and hold me. I set up an anchor in the cracks of the horizontal portion of the rock cliff and attached to them a four-foot sling. With the sling I could lower myself over the edge of the cliff hand over hand until my belay device became taught and then I would be able to rappel. Additional information: I would have to rappel with my pack and a ton of gear I had brought. The pack probably weighed about 25–30 pounds.

I got ready to rappel. I ran the single rope through my belay device (an ATC) with a locking carabiner. Everything with my harness and belay device was set up fine. The toprope was set up fine. I lowered myself over the edge of the cliff so that I was facing the cliff. My pack was hanging below me. It was attached to the belay loop on my harness and hanging between my legs. What happened next happened very quickly. I somehow managed to lose control and did not grab the brake rope. I fell completely uncontrolled and without the aid of friction created by the belay device and rope. I hit the ground after about a 50 foot fall.

Analysis
I did not back up my rappel with a prusik knot. I didn't even wrap the brake end of the rope around my leg a few times. (This little technique could have saved me from this whole situation.)

Some other factors:
- Single rope rappels create significantly less braking friction in an ATC belay device.
- I was rappelling on a 10.3mm—fairly new (not very frayed) rope.
- The actual point where the rope was anchored was about 2.5 feet down the cliff face—which meant that I would have to lower myself over the cliff edge quite a ways before my belay device became active and weight-bearing.
- The added weight of my pack (25-30 pounds) caused a significant pulling effect on me and as I lowered myself over the edge of the cliff, the added weight became quite disruptive. I had trouble with the dexterity I needed to move my body around and get into position for the rappel

I believe people could learn a few things from this accident. Back up a rappel, even if it's with the brake rope wrapped around the leg. Be very conscious of rappelling on one rope. If one must "back" off a cliff in order to make the anchors and belay device active (which everyone does), be very conscious of a backup system and how the whole rappel is going to unfold.

I believe that I am a very good climber. I'm not talking about what rating I can climb but my understanding of anchors, roped systems, climbing techniques, climbing safety and all that. I read, on a regular basis, about all these types of climbing techniques. I've been climbing since I was 17 years old, 11 years ago. I've climbed a lot and I take it very seriously. I can't believe this happened to me. I've been in very, very similar situations and understood what was required. [It] seems to me to be a culmination of overlooked, small but important points that led to a very serious accident. I guess that's a definition of an accident. (Source: Mike Porowski)

FALL ON ROCK, SOLO CLIMBING WITH NO PROTECTION
Colorado, Boulder Canyon, The Dome
On October 26, Scott Hamilton (49) lost his grip while climbing a difficult route on The Dome without ropes, safety gear, or a helmet. He fell more than 150 feet, hit a steep slope and tumbled another 100 feet into Boulder Canyon. Witnesses climbing nearby told authorities that they heard a yell, looked up, and watched him fall through the air.

It is believed he was either on King Kong or Gorilla's Delight. Both routes are rated 5.9, meaning they contain moves where only one reasonable hold exists. If Hamilton was on Gorilla's Delight when he fell, he was in the process of joining an elite and daredevil group of people who have ever climbed it without safety gear. Henry Barber once said he came closer to dying on Gorilla's Delight than any other climb he soloed.

Those who knew Hamilton say they are mourning a well-liked, intelligent, and articulate man. Since 1999, Hamilton has worked at the East Boulder Recreation Center, introducing kids ages eight to 15 to the climbing wall. Last year, he pioneered a women's wall program, now one of the center's most popular offerings. "He was always emphasizing safety, safety, safety, safety," said Ken Silva, a program manager at the center. "It wasn't like him to be without ropes." Hamilton moved to Boulder eight-and-a-half years ago from northern California. In addition to teaching climbing, he held various part-time jobs at local warehouses. Standing about six feet tall with short, peppered hair, he was the portrait of a muscular climber. He lifted weights four times a week where he worked. Often, the single man would go climbing alone. "He was very comfortable doing things a little scarier than I was," said his friend Kevin Scott. Hamilton taught Scott how to climb. Over the past three years, the two had climbed together nearly 50 times. "That's when he was happiest," Scott said. "When he was out there." (Source: From a story by Chris Barge in *The Daily Camera*, October 29, 2002)

Analysis

Invoking the name of Henry Barber in conjunction with this climb causes me to begin with a personal observation of Henry's combination of abilities. I had the pleasure of doing two climbs with him—and then watching him do a solo on-site—in Guilin, China, in 1980. (This was after our six-man team had made an attempt to do a new route on Minya Konka.) Like a pianist or dancer, part of Henry's brain structure is in his hands and feet! People who are accomplished in these fields do not have to think about what their hands (fingers) and feet should do once the head has orchestrated the series of moves to come. This, combined with the skill to suppress any feelings of panic (and strength, of course), allowed Henry to push through on routes like Gorilla's Delight.

Climbers like Scott Hamilton achieve a level of confidence, especially on familiar routes and in familiar territory, that sometimes results in a miscalculation or a reduction of focus. We also cannot help but ponder the ultimate question: Why did he attempt to solo this route? If part of his life was being a mentor to youngsters, why would he put himself in the classic "do what I say, not what I do" position?

As he chose to solo with no protection and no helmet, he also chose the possible consequences. All that can be said in conclusion is that, based on close to thirty years of compiling this report, I have found that very few experienced climbers have taken serious falls while solo climbing without protection. (Source: Jed Williamson)

MISSING/OVERDUE
Colorado, Rocky Mountain National Park

This report is the amalgamation of five different incidents that, although singularly were not significant, collectively illustrate how minor problems that can grow into much larger incidents. In 2002, 25 of 28 rescue calls at Rocky Mountain National Park were for missing/overdue parties. Between June 19 and August 18, five of these calls were for parties that were missing/overdue from attempts/ascents of the Casual Route IV-V 5.10, the most popular route on the Diamond of Longs Peak. Two of these Diamond incidents resulted in responses of park personnel beyond the trailhead because of the amount of time overdue. None of the missing/overdue persons was injured.

Similar factors were seen in the Diamond incidents, and also in many of the other missing/overdue incidents. Each of the teams had at least one person on the team who was minimally experienced for attempting a large alpine wall such as the Diamond. Some of the persons interviewed stated that most of their prior experience had been in the gymnasium. Some of the other persons, while properly experienced, were not properly acclimated for the severe climbing above 13,000 feet in elevation. Two of the teams had three and four persons, which complicated the logistics of efficient movement. At least two of the Diamond teams did not get a sufficiently early start to their climbing day.

Analysis

While none of the five overdue/missing Diamond party incidents were serious in nature, all had the potential for serious mishap. These incidents do offer us a reflection on what is necessary for success on a serious alpine big wall such as the Diamond. First, all of the climbers teamed up for a Diamond or similar big wall should have sufficient experience, including leading efficiently at free-climbing standards of 5.10 and above. All team members should have experience in climbing big walls at lesser elevations. All team members should have experience and acclimitization for undergoing serious exertion at high altitude. All team members should be proficient with direct aid techniques, self rescue, and first aid, in the event of being challenged with their own or someone else's catastrophe. Second, smaller teams usually offer the better chance of success due to the simplicity of logistics when compared with large groups in confined spaces such as small belay stances or ledges. Finally, one must constantly consider safety as the most important factor on any climb, whether in reference to fast efficient movement, proper planning in designing a sufficient acclimation period and an early start, and even partner choice as to adequate experience and proficiency levels.

The parties illustrated in these incidents were fortunate that the weather did not change or that other catastrophic events did not occur. Longs Peak can be quite unforgiving, even to the best climbers. Even when a party is properly experienced, adequately equipped, and has planned carefully, the worst scenarios might still unfold. This is what the challenge of climbing is all about. It is most important to stack the odds in your favor by pitting your skills instead of mere luck against the mountain. (Source: Jim Detterline—Longs Peak Area Ranger, and Mark Magnuson—Wild Basin District Ranger, Rocky Mountain National Park)

(Editor's Note: A correction from last year's Colorado section on the spelling of Bastille Crack. It managed to get in one report as "Bestowal" Crack—due to an auto spell checker, then being missed by proof reader.

There were two fatalities that don't appear in the Colorado narratives. One was a rappelling accident in Boulder Canyon and the other was a free fall on the Flatirons, both in February, and because both were solo, there are no details.)

FALL ON ROCK, INADEQUATE PROTECTION, POOR TECHNIQUE
New Hampshire, Cathedral Ledge, Recompense

On June 28, Bayard Russel (26) and I (Rand McNally—48) were climbing Recompense (5.9). I was leading the first pitch and we were using a double-rope technique, which I had only done once before. The first pitch is moderate (5.7) and well within my ability. I had led it before on a single rope.

It was a very hot day, and this was my first climb in my shoes since they had been resoled. I had a piece (or protection) at my feet with a shoulder-length sling attached. I could have placed a piece above my head, but the route was traversing left, so drag would be a factor—and it's a long climb requiring large pieces toward the end. There was a small ledge in the fall-zone, but I felt that if I fell, I would clear it. I made a thin, slabby face-move to the left and slipped in such a way that I sled straight down, contacting the ledge with the outside edge of my left foot. I suffered a compound ankle fracture.

We initiated self-rescue, and as we were rappelling through the woods and talus, we were met by a local guide and members of the Mountain Rescue Service, who were climbing nearby.

Analysis

The long sling was superfluous and left me with more distance to fall. (I needed) better protection and better use of rope technique, and better assessment of the conditions. The heat made me sweaty and new soles made my shoes less sensitive, so what was normally a moderately difficult move, this day I was unable to complete. (Source: Rand McNally)

Recompense is one of those climbs whose level of difficulty can be deceiving, especially for less experienced leaders. The pitch is very long—a full 60 meters, and requires lots of gear. It also traverses gradually from right to left with the crux of the climb being in the last 30 feet. There are also a lot of fixed pitons, but all of them are old and should be backed up. Many climbers fail to protect adequately here. (Source: Al Hospers)

FALL ON ROCK, ROPE SEVERED
New Hampshire, Eagle Cliff, Shape Shifters

Steve Dupuis and Jon Sykes, both experienced climbers, were attempting to free a climb they had put up as an A4 aid climb some time before. On October

14, they met at the parking lot to sort gear. They had a 60 meter, 10.2 mm and 60 meter, 9 mm ropes. It was cold and there was a little ice on the cliff as they walked in.

Jon led the first pitch and did a slight variation to the original. It was a slow lead and the rock was a little slick. He belayed at a two-bolt anchor about 100 feet up. He fixed the climbing rope and Steve jugged 30–40 feet to a stance at a ledge where he noticed that the sheath of the rope he was jugging on was frayed about ten feet above him. He reset the nut that Jon had placed, clipped in with a sling and Jon threw down an end of the 9 mm. After tying in, Steve free-climbed the remainder of the pitch. When he got to where the 10.2 rope was frayed, he tied in above it with a figure 8 knot and continued climbing, belayed on the 9 mm. At the belay he tied off and hauled up the 10.2. They observed that sheath was cut on the rope and there was about one inch of exposed core. At that time they looked the entire rope over, except where Jon was tied in, and it looked like there were no other problems. They cut the 10.2 above the fray and threw it down.

Steve tied back into the end of the 10.2 mm. At that time he was still tied into the 9 mm, but was not belayed on it; HOWEVER, the 9 mm was tied off to the anchor! They talked about where the bolt should go. On the original A4 version of the second pitch, Jon had taken a line that angled steeply off to the right. Steve free climbed three or four moves off the belay. He found what looked like a good bolt placement but there was no gear between it and the belay. He was 8-10 feet to the right and about a foot above the belay at a stance on a four to six inch ledge that was leaning out. He got into his aiders using a BD hook on an in-cut ledge about four feet above his feet. He tried to drill a bolt with a small electric hand drill, but couldn't apply enough pressure using only one hand, so he sent the drill back to Jon on the 9 mm. Steve wanted to get a pin in a crack, but he was unable to reach it from his stance. They were talking to each other all the time and Steve was saying that he was going to move back to his left. As he was switching his feet in his aiders, the hook popped. Steve expected only a short fall and he anticipated hitting the ledge. As he pendulumned to his left, he felt a jerk and "saw the rope go white." He knew he was falling.

He hit a ledge about 30 feet below the belay with his left side, somersaulted and tumbled, continuing another 70–90 feet to the ground, landing on his back. His Ecrin Roc helmet came off on impact and landed 40 feet away. Steve remained conscious both throughout the fall and after. He and Jon called back and forth to confirm that he was still alive. Steve was still tied into the 9 mm rope and had to untie it before Jon could rappel down to help. The rope was under a lot of tension and when Steve let it go, it jerked away. As he had tied into the 9 mm at least 30 feet up during the initial climbing on the first pitch, the stretch in the rope helped lessen his impact on the ground. In addition, he was wearing three layers of clothing, top and bottom, and had an almost-full Camelback HOG on his back containing additional gear.

Analysis

Dupuis has been rock climbing for over 17 years. This was the first time he has fallen this far and this hard. "It's all part of the hazards (of rock climbing)," Dupuis said. "The system was supposed to take the weight of the fall and I guess it's an unlucky catastrophic failure. The rope was under two years old and in mint condition. It was babied." Amazingly enough Steve only had relatively minor injuries and has completely recovered. He has returned to climbing and guiding.

So these were two strong climbers with many years of experience between them, but despite the fact that they had already had one rope badly cut, neither climber noticed that the belay ledge on the second pitch had extremely sharp edges. When Steve fell, his rope remained taut as he pendulumned, and that rope, under tension, scraped along the edge of the belay ledge and was cut as if by a serrated knife.

Forgetting to untie from the 9mm rope may have saved Steve's life, though his helmet and clothing played a role too. However, we can't say for sure that using double ropes would have prevented the accident. It's possible that two ropes under tension from the fall could have cut as easily the one, with disastrous results.

If climbers know of or discover en route sharp edges that could slice a rope, they should pad the edge, or place protection that will direct the rope away from the edge. Trying to free an aid climb requires a bit of thought about protection and the line of the original route—especially if there are sharp edges to consider.

Finally, if you are freeing an aid route, tying into your haul line, and clipping the other end and middle of the rope to the belay (an old aid climber's trick) as a worst-case backup, never hurts. (Sources: Al Hospers, Jed Eliades, and Alexander MacInnes, in *The Caledonian Record*, October 16, 2002)

AVALANCHE, POOR POSITION, INADEQUATE EQUIPMENT
New Hampshire, Mount Washington, Tuckerman Ravine

Tom Striker and Tony Tulip, hiked up in to Tuckerman Ravine on November 29. The first in the ravine, they hiked to the base of an open book on the right of center and decided to climb it straight up. Tom belayed at an exposed bulge and put in thee screws equalized with a cordelette. He observed what looked like a lot of snow-loading on the slope in front of him, before the next steep section. At that time three other climbers (Tom Burke, Rick Doucette, and Matt Coutre) showed up at base of their climb, geared up and started soloing. One climber was on the right and two on the left side of the book. Tony, the second, climbed up to the belay and around the same time the three soloists joined up on a slope above them. At this time Striker and Tony didn't like what was happening and decided to bail. Tony continued up a little and traversed right to a position near the Tuckerman Ravine Trail.

The soloists continued up in the direction of the Lip, following paths of least resistance. Two went left and one right. Around this time they touched off several surface slides. All three climbers at this time were still within sight of Striker, who was still at the three-screw belay. All of a sudden one of the soloists, Tom Burke, fell from the Lip area, tumbling approximately 100 feet and coming to rest about 40 feet above Striker at the belay. For unknown reasons, the other two soloists continued to climb. After lying there for a minute, Tom Burke shook himself, stood up and yelled, "I'm OK!" to his companions. He appeared dazed and started to down climb and move toward Tony, near the trail. Tom Striker, at the belay, said to wait for him and they would move together. Around this time he also noticed that two more climbers (Scott Sandburg and Richard Doucette) were below him at the base of the climb next to their packs, getting gear together and roping up. They did not seem to have any awareness of what was going on above them. The two soloists were on or above the Lip when someone yelled, "Avalanche!" Tom Striker at his belay ducked down, grabbed the cordelette and amazingly the avalanche passed over him.

Once things cleared, Striker could see a debris field extending 100-plus yards down the slope. He lowered off a screw and the search began for survivors. The two upper soloists had ridden the avalanche all the way down from the Lip. Matt was unscathed, Richard was partially buried and suffered a broken shoulder. Tom Burke, who had just survived a 100-foot fall, was swept away and buried, suffering fatal trauma. Neither Scott nor Richard, at the base of the book, had any indication that an avalanche was coming. They were standing three to four feet apart and Richard was closer to the wall. Scott was swept away and buried while Richard was untouched.

Richard was able to uncover Matt, Rick, and Scott very quickly. Unfortunately Scott suffered fatal injuries and was never conscious after the slide. Tom Burke took longer to find, but also suffered the same fate. Even though all of those buried were found fairly quickly, the deaths were not caused by suffocation but by trauma.

Analysis

Tuckerkman Ravine is notorious for avalanches and yet is very popular for early season ice climbing. At the time of this accident the posted avalanche danger was MODERATE. As many climbers have said, if they didn't climb in those conditions, they probably wouldn't climb at all.

None of the climbers had beacons, probes, or shovels. (Source: Al Hospers and Roger Damon)

(Editor's Note: Even with "moderate" avalanche conditions, where you are positioned in relationship to other climbers is an important consideration. These climbers were in each other's fall-line.

The records show that twelve people have died in avalanches on Mount Washington in the last 150 years. Sunday, just two days after the deaths of Burke and Sandberg, four more climbers in Tuckerman, two of whom had participated in the rescue, were swept down the mountain in another avalanche. Three escaped unhurt, but one woman's head was buried, causing neck injuries.)

FALL ON ROCK—HANDHOLD PULLED OUT, APPARENTLY FAILED TO TEST HOLD, OFF ROUTE, INADEQUATE PROTECTION
New Mexico, Sandia Mountain Wilderness, Muralla Grande

On May 8, two resident physicians set out to climb Warpy Moople (5.9-.10, III), an eight pitch, 816 foot route on Muralla Grande, one of the major formations in the Sandia Mountain Wilderness outside of Albuquerque. On the first pitch the leader placed a small TCU, and then began a mantle move approximately fifteen feet above the piece. The belayer recalls that the leader was off-route to the left of the climb. The leader was fully committed to the move when the rock he was mantling onto pulled out. He fell for thirty five to forty feet before his belayer caught him.

The leader fell backwards striking the right side of his body, but also hit the left side of his head hard enough to break the strapping system of the Ecrin Roc helmet and knock him unconscious for a moment. He suffered a severe concussion. He recalls, "I only remember eating burritos at the Frontier Restaurant and then waking up in my hospital room…not even the emergency room."

His partner attempted to call for a help on his cell phone, but the increasing amount of radio frequency radiation emitted from Sandia Crest renders cell phones and two way radios almost useless, so they were unable to use the phone for several hours. The belayer lowered the leader and was able to help him walk out. He finally reached 911 by cell phone three hours after the incident and local rescue resources were activated but were not needed because the two men were able to hike out without assistance. (Submitted by J. Marc Beverly, PA/Paramedic, Albuquerque Mountain Rescue Council)

Analysis

There are some tantalizing details missing here, but there seems to be a basic message: Test your holds. Last year, a disproportionate number of "handhold (or foothold) came loose" incidents were reported. It also seems that more than a small TCU should have been considered to protect the first moves.

A side-bar is the comment relating to the victim's short term memory: Personally, I hope my last memory is a little more exciting than eating burritos. (Source: Jed Williamson)

(Editor's Note: Warpy Moople claimed the lives of three climbers in 1996, the day before a National Forest closure due to extreme fire danger. See ANAM 1997)

FALL WHILE DESCENDING—INADEQUATE EQUIPMENT (CLIMBING ROPE, RAPPEL DEVICE, HARNESS, BRAIN CELLS)
New Mexico, Jemez Mountains, Yoyo Pit

On May 16, a man and his girlfriend were on an excursion in the Santa Fe National Forest, which had been closed due to extreme fire danger. Yoyo Pit is a popular spot for vertical rope work as the pit is straight vertical until about half way down where it bells-out and turns to complete free-hang. Formed by a large gas bubble while the volcanic flow was cooling it is approximately thirty feet in diameter and has much lose rock.

The man apparently dropped his cell phone into the 170-foot pit. He decided to get some equipment from his vehicle and rig a descent with a tow rope, a come-along, a pulley, and two ropes not rated for rope work of any kind. The tow-rope was girth hitched to a sturdy tree and the come-along was wrapped once around the tree and clipped back to itself near the end of the tow rope. This is where he had a pulley clipped to the come-along with the descending rope running through the pulley. The tie-off was with five half hitches and the then the rope went down into the abyss. The end of the first rope was tied to the second rope in order to reach the bottom. The two ropes were tied together with a series of half-hitches.

The man told his girlfriend that he knew what he was doing and that he had done this type of thing before. He used two sets of gloves to grasp the rope with but did not have a harness of any sort and did not use any sort of friction device to slow his descent. He merely went hand over hand down into the pit, according to his girlfriend. She also said he made it about half way down before the bell of the bottom (estimated at approximately seventy to eighty feet), and then he lost his grip and fell backwards. She reported that he was laughing on the way down.

After he hit the bottom he apparently continued to laugh and stated that he thought he broke his arm. A minute later he said he could not move and could not feel his back, that all was numb. The girlfriend went for help to Santa Fe since there was no cell phone. She managed to get to a pay phone to call 911. Fire Department and Search and Rescue were activated. By the time rescue personnel made it to the scene the man had died.

There were rope burns on the man's gloves and his arms. He had bilateral leg fractures, a broken arm and died from internal injuries, either internal hemorrhage or neurogenic shock. (J. Marc Beverly, PA/Paramedic, Albuquerque Mountain Rescue Council)

Analysis

While this is not considered to be a "legitimate" climbing accident, it illustrates how quickly people with no experience can get in trouble trying to become climbers. In addition to the technical mistakes here, it seems this fellow appears to have been a few tools short of a full box.

Unfortunately, the press will portray an incident such as this as proof that climbing is a dangerous sport. (Sources: J. Marc Beverly, PA/Paramedic—Albuquerque Mountain Rescue Council, and Jed Williamson)

FALL OR SLIP ON ROCK
North Carolina, Pilot Mountain State Park

On Friday, February 22, I (J.W. Peterson) was walking along the cliff top when I heard Brian Zimmerman (20) yelling and sliding down the rock face below the Ledge Springs Trail. I called to the climbers on the trail below and asked them if anyone was hurt. Chris Jones (20) called back and said, "Yes," that Brian had sustained a head and neck injury, and a broken leg. From my vantage point above, I could see Jones administering first aid to Zimmerman. I left the scene to call 911. My call informed me that Surry

County EMS and Pilot Mountain Rescue were en route. I gave them the specific location of the accident and waited for them to arrive. Upon arrival, I accompanied rescue squad members to the top of the cliff where Zimmerman had fallen.

While leaving this site I was approached by Jessica Riley (20) and Zach Groff (20) who had been climbing with Zimmerman. I asked them to explain what had happened. They said that Zimmerman was free-soloing to the top of the cliff to set up a top rope climb. As he reached the top, he could not figure out how to go any higher. Advice from another climber was unsuccessful. Zimmerman slipped and fell approximately 30 feet.

Zimmerman was carried out by rescue squad members and transported to Baptist Hospital in Winston Salem, NC. Zimmerman suffered a laceration to the head that required several stitches, a broken right elbow and a broken lower right leg. (Source: J. W. Pearson, Pilot Mountain State Park)

Analysis
Pilot Mountain is a very popular and well established top rope climbing area. All climbs are easily accessible via the Ledge Springs Trail which runs along the top and bottom of the cliff. Climbers usually set up their climbs before descending to the base of the cliff or access the cliff top via the Three Bears Gully. The area is also known for loose rock and overhanging exits. Why the climber chose to free-solo to access the top is unknown. Free-solo climbing comes with increased inherent risks. (Source: Aram Attarian)

FALL ON ROCK, PROTECTION CAME OUT, NO HARD HAT
North Carolina, Linville Gorge, North Carolina Wall
On September 8, Colin Treiber, (20), and his partner were climbing Bumblebee Buttress (5.8), located on the North Carolina Wall in the Linville Gorge Wilderness Area. Treiber, an experienced climber, lost his balance before he was able to clip into his fifth piece of protection and began to fall. The rock where the fourth piece of protection was placed broke, causing the piece to come out. His first, second and third protection pieces remained but did not prevent him from hitting the base of the route. Additional reports suggest that he fell on the upper part of the first pitch well above his last piece of protection. When his last piece blew, it caused him to invert, striking the back of his head against the wall. A broken neck and concussion to the head were the major injuries. He was not wearing a helmet. CPR initiated by his partner was unsuccessful

Experienced climbers at the scene said that Treiber was using the appropriate equipment and it was in good working order. Over 40 personnel from Burke County Emergency Services, Burke County EMS Special Operations Team, Jonas Ridge Fire and First Responders, Burke County Rescue Squad, Lake James Fire Department, Oak Hill Fire Department, Burke County REACT, North Carolina Outward Bound School, and Linville Central Rescue were involved in the body recovery. (Sources: Sharon McBrayer, *The News Herald*, September 9, 2002, and Aram Attarian)

Analysis

I went into the Gorge with knowledge of the accident but not sure where it happened. When I arrived at the base of Bumblebee Buttress, my whole day changed. I saw two pieces of gear still in place on the route, the first piece, a well-placed .75 Camalot. It was about 15 feet up. The second was a #8 Metolius cam. It was about 20 feet higher, right below the crux of the first pitch. Both were in good rock with long slings. I saw no fifth piece. I had planned on soloing the route, but only went up as far as the gear I could see from the ground—40 feet or so, not quite up into the corner system.

On the first ledge at the base of the route I found a rope bag and a "mashed up" #4 Metolius cam. The cam looked as though it had been pulled through the crack. The trigger was pushed up against the cam head and the head itself was "chewed up." With the stem slightly bent, it looked like it had taken a small amount of force before it popped. It was not in good working order. My guess is that it was the second piece to fail.

In between the .75 and the #8 Metolius, I found a damaged .5 Camalot lying in the crack. The .5 showed signs of great stress. It looked as though it was placed horizontally. The cam head was slightly mashed on one side, but the stem was bent over like a piece of elbow macaroni. The cable was crushed and frayed, showing signs of significant force spread out over the entire stem. It looked as though it was placed on top of and behind a blocky feature. The sling of the cam was frayed on the clip in end and looked as though it had been melted with a hot iron on the side that would have been in contact with the rock.

My guess is Colin lost his footing trying to clip his fifth piece and fell (possibly upside down) 20-25 feet onto the .5 Camalot. I'm not sure whether or not he collided with the rock before the placement failed or after, but given the amount of force the .5 Camalot looks to have taken, it suggests that it happened after, causing the rock around the placement to explode and fall down onto Colin. The #4 Metolius cam seems not to have held either, also due to rock quality. There was a significant amount scaring caused by rocks about the size of a soccer ball low on the route. Colin's fall was then arrested by the #8 Metolius a few feet off the deck. All in all the fall was probably around 80-90 feet.

With all this said, here is what I think we can learn from this tragic accident. Always wear a helmet while climbing in the Gorge, try to use passive protection as much as possible around hollow or questionable rock features, and be extremely cautious of ledge-fall potential. (Source: From observations by Pat Goodman, a local climber)

FALLING ICE—FALL ON ICE
New York, Adirondacks, Poke-O-Monshine

Ice on the first pitch of the popular 160-foot climb "Positive Thinking" broke off Poke-O-Moonshine Friday and crashed to the ground, taking an Ontario climber with it.

Kevin Bailey (34) was about 135 feet up and anchoring himself to the east side of the mountain when the ice split and detached. His climbing partner, Jason Kuruc, also of Ontario, stood below with the belay device, waiting to begin his assent. After the crash, Kuruc left the mountain to get help, and returned to assist emergency workers, who attempted cardiopulmonary resuscitation, but could not revive the man.

Eventually, Kuruc was taken to CVPH Medical Center in Plattsburgh where he was treated for minor injuries and released.

Analysis

For a majority of the winter, the 85-degree pitch on Poke-O-Moonshine has been stellar for climbing. Ed Palen, a guide for Adirondack Rock and River Guide Service, said more climbers than ever attempted the nearly vertical climb this year, which sits on a giant face of rock about a mile long.

"It looks like in two or three days it went from a lot of good ice climbing to not much at all," he said, after hearing about the accident Friday evening. Palen said that with the number of climbers and the good conditions, he wasn't surprised an accident occurred but didn't expect anything tragic.

"The climb was very safe and good for the past three weeks," said Palen, who's guided it a handful of times in the past two weeks, to some clients who've been waiting years to get a piece of it. "I've never seen more people climbing than this year."

"We were seeing some scary things this year," he said. "They heard Positive Thinking was in and everyone was rushing to it." He said warm, rainy days took a toll on the ice, which streaks down the mountainside, creating four or five different climbs for the year.

"It's still the most sought after ice-climb in New York State," Palen said. "People will drive six, eight, ten hours if they hear that it's in. It's still considered one of the best climbs and certainly the best-known climb in the Adirondacks. [It's] something you aim your climbing career for."

He said color, sound, and ambient air temperature all give clues as to whether a climb is safe or not. But Palen, active in the sport for more than 20 years, said the only way to know is through experience. "There are young climbers with braver attitudes...doing harder things earlier with not quite the experience in judgments," he said. (Source: From an article by M'chelle Peterson)

VARIOUS FALLS ON ROCK, PROTECTION PULLED OUT, INADEQUATE PROTECTION, AND RAPPEL ERRORS
New York, Mohonk Preserve, Shawangunks

There were 29 incidents reported for 2002. More than half were injuries sustained from lead climbing. In eight of the leader falls, protection pulled out. In seven others, leaders were "run out" in that they had too much slack in the belay system, which resulted in long falls to ledges, impacting the cliff, or grounding out. In the four top-rope incidents, the climbers were injured because they made pendulum swings when they fell.

There were five bouldering incidents—which is an increase from previous years. These falls were from ten to twenty feet off the deck with inadequate spotting or padding as a contributing cause.

One injury of note resulted when a lead climber pulled a two-cinder block sized rock loose and almost completely severed his right index finger. He was able to rappel and self-evacuate. The finger was successfully reattached.

One of the two rappel incidents happened in November when a climber was down-climbing to a rappel point. As his protection popped out due to "mushy ice" lining the crack, he fell fifteen feet, resulting in a fractured tibia and fibula.

The average age of the climbers injured was 30, and 20 out of the 28 were males. The climbing routes were mostly of moderate difficulty. (Source: Mohonk Preserve)

FALL INTO CREVASSE, UNABLE TO SELF-ARREST, INADEQUATE PROTECTION, POOR POSITION
Oregon, Mount Hood, Standard Route

On May 30 at 8:30 a.m., there were climbers both ascending and descending the mountain along the standard route. A team of four climbers (Team A) was on its way down. Leading the way was HS (43), followed by CK (43), RR (49), and BW (50). All climbers were separated by about 35 feet of rope. All four members of Team A had reached the summit, and after a rest break were in the process of descending. Of the four, the most experienced climbers were HS and CK. BW was an active climber with less experience, and RR was on his first climb.

Below Team A, also descending, was a two-man climbing team (Team B), consisting of TH (46) and JB (63). Team C, consisting of two rope-teams, was working its way up the mountain. The first rope-team contained JP (39), CoJ (15), and JM (26), all of whom were about 20-40 feet above the Bergschrund crevasse. The second rope-team contained DB (28), SM (33), ClJ (48), and CH (33). This rope-team was about five feet below the crevasse ascending the mountain behind the first rope-team of Team C.

For an unknown reason, the top two members of Team A lost their footing and were unable to arrest their fall. These two individuals subsequently pulled the other two members of their four-person team into an uncontrolled slide. Party A fell out of control until their team's rope became entangled with the rope of Party B, who were then pulled into the slide. All six members of parties A and B eventually hit the first rope-team of party C.

All of these subjects involved in the fall went into the crevasse below them. Mr. William Ward, Mr. Richard Read, and Mr. John Biggs were killed. Mr. Harry Slutter, Mr. Chris Kern, Mr. Tom Hillman, and Mr. Jeremiah Moffitt were critically injured, while Mr. Jeff Pierce and Mr. Cole Joiner received minor injuries.

A mountain rescue operation was initiated and the injured survivors were extricated from the crevasse and transported to area hospitals.

Analysis

At the time of this incident it was full daylight conditions, the sky reported to be clear, an occasional light wind, the temperature at about freezing. At the Timberline Lodge at 8:00 a.m., the temperature was 52 degrees F and the average wind speed nine mph. Since the snow surface conditions at 10,900 feet were reported as frozen, crampons were required and provided good purchase by step-climbing in the snow.

The bergschrund was visible, there was a snow bridge across it, some climbers were choosing to cross over the snow bridge, some to detour around it. Above the bergschrund is the steepest part of this climb, continuing upward through a steep gully, several outcroppings of rock named "The Pearly Gates," and then a short ascent to the summit of the mountain, the high point 11, 239 feet.

Mr. Butler later said that he was pausing to give Pierce's team a few minutes to get back on the ridge before Butler's group began the detour around the crevasse. At this time the two highest climbers of the involved parties, Bill Ward and Rick Read, lost their footing and fell. This happened very fast, Chris Kern said that he saw a blur in his field of vision; it happened so fast that he did not remember any verbal warning from the falling climbers.

Mr. Kern went into the arrest position as soon as he saw the blur, but the weight of the other two climbers pulled him right off the mountain.

All four were properly equipped for the climb and in good physical condition. Mr. Slutter, in the lead climbing down, had considerable experience in alpine mountain climbing, as did Mr. Kern behind him. Mr. Ward in the trail position also had experience in alpine mountain climbing. Mr. Read, who was in good health, was on his first alpine climb, and the team of four had spent considerable time practicing climbing techniques prior to starting. He had no problems on the climb up the mountain to the summit.

Several lessons can be learned from this incident.

1. Climbing on steep snow or ice, roped without the use of anchors, can, under certain circumstances, be a dangerous practice. It may be unrealistic to presume that a climber who has fallen and is unable to self-arrest will be able to be stopped by another climber or climbers set in self-arrest position. The forces involved can simply be too great for other members of the rope-team to arrest the fall. In these cases, the rope becomes a liability to the group, ensuring that a fall will involve numerous climbers, rather than only the climber who initially slipped. Generally speaking, if a snow or ice slope is steep enough to require a rope, then it is probably steep enough to require using anchors.

2. Positioning is an important aspect of climbing. Climbers must be aware of hazards above (be they falling rock, ice, cornices, avalanches, or other climbers). It is interesting to note that in this incident, the climbers with the worst injuries were the ones who fell the longest overall distance. The climbers who were simply knocked into the crevasse generally did not sustain life-threatening injuries. However, in the weeks following the acci-

dent, many climbers were seen taking a climbing line that took them directly underneath the rotten gendarmes that rain ice and rock down the route, instead of circumventing the crevasse and returning to the apex of the Hogs Back where rock and icefall is lower. Climbers should evaluate hazards holistically; in this case it is probably safer to stay on the ridge rather than climbing under rotten rock for an extended period of time.

3. Climbers should consider climbing unroped on moderate terrain where the risk of a fall is low and the risk from objective hazards, such as falling rock, ice, or other climbers, is high. The use of ropes and anchors will slow a climbing party down and may restrict individuals options for evasive action should an emergency occur.

4. Be aware of the risks of helicopters in mountainous environments. Helicopters should only be used when there is no other practical resort, where lives are at stake, and time is of the essence. Climbers may joke about calling in air support for blisters or a pizza drop, but the fact of the matter is that helicopters can set up extremely dangerous conditions and lives can become at risk when they are used in the mountains. Helicopters cannot be depended on to perform in all conditions. Rescuers and rescuees must always make contingency plans, even if a helicopter is initially available to assist in the rescue.

5. Pay attention and follow the instructions of mountain rescuers; they are trained in the risks and techniques of conducting mountain rescues. In this case, several bystanders and some members of the involved climbing teams assisted with the rescue efforts. This assistance was extremely helpful and appreciated and may have saved lives. However, when rescuers directed everyone not directly involved with the hoist operation to clear the area underneath the helicopter, some bystanders declined to descend. As a result, far too many lives were put at risk when the helicopter crashed. (Sources: Steve Rollins—Portland Mountain Rescue, and Tim Baily—Criminalist Investigator)

(Editor's Note: The story of the helicopter crash was thoroughly covered by television and several newspapers. Details are not provided here for that reason and because it was not a mountain climbing accident.)

FALL ON ROCK, INADEQUATE PROTECTION, BELAYER NOT ANCHORED
Oregon, Smith Rock, Spiderman

Nathan Sanborn (27) was climbing the first pitch of Spiderman, a four star classic climb rated 5.7 by Alan Watts (trad gear to three inches) when he slipped off about three feet above his last protection and fell an estimated 12 to 15 feet due to rope stretch and an inadvertent dynamic belay. The toe of one foot struck a bulge on the low-angled rock, hyper-extending his foot and breaking a bone in his ankle. Additional tissue damage was done as well, and the injury was very painful.

Nathan was lowered off about 50 feet and the party called 911 for assistance. Redmond Fire and Rescue arrived in about one hour and Deschutes

County Sheriff's SAR somewhat later. Nathan was lowered down the scree in a belayed stokes litter, carried to the trailhead and transported to hospital.

Analysis

Nathan suggests that lead climbers set protection as high as possible before attempting a difficult move. His equalized #1 Camalot and medium hex held his fall, but the stretch of the long rope and a dynamic belay turned a seeming seven footer into a 12 to 15 foot fall. The belayer, standing back from the wall, was pulled forward into the wall, contributing to the length of the fall. Nathan, about 200 pounds, states that in the future, he will make sure that his belayer is anchored.

Low-angled climbs can be more deceiving than vertical rock. (Source: Robert Speik)

FALL ON ROCK–LOWERING ERROR, NO HARD HAT
Oregon, Smith Rock State Park, Left Slab Crack.

On November 29, Kathy Lee and her friend Becky Hsu (both 27) were meeting some new friends at The Dihedrals at Smith Rock. The friends were late, so Kathy and Becky decided to warm up with Left Slab Crack rated 5.4 two stars by Alan Watts in his *Climber's Guide to Smith Rock*. Kathy topped out and asked her friend to lower her. She realized the rope was short for this climb but expected Becky to hold her so she could finish the descent with a fourth-class scramble to the ground. The end of the rope whipped through Becky's belay device and Kathy fell about 30 vertical feet down the route to the ground. Without a helmet, she was bleeding profusely from a head wound.

EMS professionals were summoned by a nearby cell phone. She was stabilized and carried by the waiting ambulance to St. Charles Medical Center, kept overnight, and released with a bruised kidney and lung and scalp lacerations. She is "lucky and well" and climbing "more carefully" again.

Analysis

Typically, the belayer is concentrating on the climber being lowered, failing to mind the remaining belay rope. Sport climbers typically do not tie into the bottom end of the top belay rope. Tying a stopper knot or tying the rope into the sport rope bag can prevent this kind of incident. (Source: Robert Speik)

RAPPEL FAILURE–INADEQUATE KNOT
Utah, Zion National Park, Spaceshot

On May 21, Roeslain Tamin (35) fell 180 feet to his death while rappelling from the popular climbing route Spaceshot in Zion National Park. Evidence and interviews lead to the following sequence of events.

Tamin and his climbing partner Richard Connors (29) had climbed the first four pitches of Spaceshot on May 20, then descended, fixing lines on the way. On May 21, they returned and ascended their fixed lines to the top of the fourth pitch. Due to approaching weather, they decided to retreat and take their ropes down with them. Tamin rappelled to the ledge on top of the second pitch followed by Connors. The two then prepared for the final 60 meter rappel to the ground. Tamin walked a short distance over to their fixed rope at the anchor, out of view of Connors. Tamin took the weight off the end of the fixed rope by clove-hitching it to a carabiner clipped to the anchor webbing. Connors pulled down a rope from the just-completed rappel, then threw the end of it to Tamin. Tamin then presumably tied the two rope ends together. Connors then fed the rest of the rope to Tamin, who in turn put it over the edge. Tamin began his rappel while Connors was coiling rope approximately ten feet away. They were separated by a boulder large enough to partially obstruct Connors' view of Tamin. Tamin probably fell shortly after going on rappel. He was found with both ropes running properly through his rappel device, with approximately ten feet of each rope above the device. But there was no evidence that the ropes had been tied together.

Analysis

Tamin and Connors had been climbing partners for eight years and tended to tie similar knots. Connors stated that they both commonly tied a figure eight knot with the tails on the same side and with an overhand backup as their primary rappel knot. Both trusted this knot but had not tested its limitations. This knot was used because of its tendency not to get stuck when pulled from below, as happens with many other knots. In this instance Tamin *may* have tied the knot with tails shorter than usual. But a backup knot was *probably* not used. These are plausible speculations due to the length of this rappel being the same as their ropes—60 meters. The lower you exit the rappel the easier the terrain becomes, and a notation made on their route description by Tamin to the effect that, "Ropes barely reach, go left of stance."

It would seem unlikely that Tamin neglected to tie the two ropes together given that the ropes were found threaded properly through his rappel device. Non-scientific tests performed on the knot in question showed several important things. When weighted, this knot will invert; if the knot is not dressed properly, it comes untied significantly more easily than will a properly dressed knot. When tied with short tails and cycled (repeated weighting and unweighting), the tails can be brought into the knot body, causing the knot to unravel.

The ropes used during this accident were sent to Black Diamond's lab in Salt Lake City, where this knot (as well as a standard overhand rappel knot) was tested using their Satec Universal Testing Machine. Tests showed that the figure eight knot inverted at loads two-thirds that of the overhand, an untightened figure eight inverted at about a 30 percent lower load than one well tightened. Conclusions of Paul Tusting, BD Quality Assurance Manager, were that, "…either the knot was tied incorrectly or it was extremely loose. The testing also demonstrates that if a well dressed figure eight with long tails were used with these ropes, a field failure of the knot is extremely unlikely. Lastly, this testing indicates that the overhand (tails on same side) is superior in strength to the figure eight (tails on same side) when well dressed and tightened." (Source: Kevin Killlian, SAR Coordinator, Zion National Park)

(Editor's Note: Fewer rappelling accidents have been reported in the last decade or so. On the other hand, lowering accidents are on the increase. The common reason for both is inattentiveness to the familiar and obvious, even among experienced climbers.)

LIGHTNING
Utah, Lone Peak

On July 26, Trent (28) and Alexis Pabst (23) were killed by a lightning strike on the summit of Lone Peak. Together with Trent's younger brother Tyler (18), the couple had climbed The Open Book, a five-pitch 5.7 route that leads straight to the 11,253-foot summit. Tyler led the final pitch. After belaying Trent up, he went to scout out a spot to shelter from the approaching storm while Trent belayed Alexis. Tyler also had time to make an eerie entry in the summit log, in which he noted the oncoming storm clouds.

At the time of the strike, Alexis had just completed the climb and untied. She and Trent were together in a small alcove at the top of the route just below the summit, while Tyler was about ten feet away. Tyler was knocked down by the blast but uninjured. Panicked, he looked at the two unresponsive climbers without touching them, then raced out for help. Five hours later, he arrived at the Bell's Canyon trailhead, having taken a longer and more difficult descent-route than he intended.

The two victims were evacuated by highline from the summit to a point lower on the summit ridge, then lowered to a meadow at about 10,800 feet, where they were loaded on board a helicopter and flown to Salt Lake City.

Analysis

The summit of Lone Peak is a room-sized pinnacle in the middle of a completely exposed ridge line. There aren't any good spots to wait out a thunderstorm on the ridge, but anywhere would have been better than the summit itself. Once the three climbers had committed to starting the last pitch, they didn't have much choice but to try to finish it and get off the peak before the storm arrived.

The Pabsts had suffered extensive burns and blast injuries and probably would not have survived. However, lightning strike victims who appear dead may in fact be in ventricular fibrillation or simply have stopped breathing. CPR can restore cardiac rhythm if it is started right away, and AR has frequently worked on victims who have just stopped breathing. An added note: With multiple lightning strike victims, triage should be the opposite of normal; that is, treat apparent fatalities first and deal with wounded victims later. (Source: Tom Moyer—Salt Lake County Sheriff's SAR)

FALL ON ROCK, PROTECTION PULLED OUT—OLD PITON
Utah, Little Cottonwood Canyon, Gate Buttress

On November 19, "Mike" (44) fell while leading the second pitch of Perhaps, a two-pitch 5.7 route at the Gate Buttress in Little Cottonwood Canyon. The end of the second pitch is a long horizontal traverse. It's an under-cling in a wide crack for the hands and low-angled friction for the feet. Mike had placed a #4 Camalot at the beginning of the traverse and had clipped an old fixed piton about 15 feet later. Another 15 feet out from the piton, he stopped and looked for the chains. As he straightened up a bit to look, his feet skated out and he fell. The piton pulled, and Mike pendulumned about 60 feet across the low-angled granite until he hit a small ledge, suffering fractures in five lumbar vertebrae, both feet, and both ankles. His partners, "Jim" and "Colin," were able to lower him back to the anchors from there, then re-rig and lower him to the ground.

SAR team members met them at the base of the route. Mike was immobilized in a bean-bag vacuum splint, lowered down five or six pitches of steep scree to the road, and then transported by ground ambulance to the hospital.

Analysis

Old fixed pitons should always be viewed with suspicion and tested. Go ahead and clip them but place good protection as soon after as you can. Mike also feels that there was a lot of slack in the rope because of rope-drag. The second pitch of Perhaps is long and twisting, with lots of ledges and flakes to snag the rope. The leader needs to choose protection placements and runner lengths carefully and consider the path of the rope to minimize these problems. Mike was wearing a helmet, and it did receive a few knocks during the fall. (Source: Tom Moyer—Salt Lake County Sheriff's SAR)

FALL ON SNOW, WEATHER, EXPOSURE, MOVING TOO SLOWLY
Washington, Mount Ranier, Liberty Ridge

On May 29, Mount Rainier National Park communications received a 911 cell phone call from a climbing team at St. Elmo's Pass. They were requesting a rescue for Andreas Kurth, another climber who reported having an accident near Liberty Cap the night before. Andreas just descended the Winthrop Glacier solo after his team, Cornelius Beilharz, Grit Kleinschmidt, and Keeta Owens, encountered serious trouble during a storm. Kurth reported that Beilharz was already dead from a fall and that the condition of the other two women was unknown. Andreas had last seen them in an exposed snow cave, hypothermic, near Liberty Cap.

The Kurth team had summited Liberty Ridge the night before, close to 6:00 p.m. They became disoriented while trying to descend from Liberty Cap to the Winthrop Glacier in a fierce storm with whiteout conditions. After unsuccessfully locating the Winthrop Glacier, the team then attempted to set up tents. However, the winds were too strong and made the task impossible. Still disoriented, the team then proceeded to dig snow caves.

Upon doing so, they encountered an impassable ice layer three feet below the surface. Unbeknownst to the team, the snow caves were being constructed atop a steep ice slope, just southeast of Liberty Cap, and fully exposed to the weather.

Unable to penetrate the ice, Kurth used the remains of a tent and the beginnings of a snow cave to erect a makeshift shelter for him and Kleinschmidt. Beilharz and Owens were attempting the same. Kurth and Kleinschmidt took cover in their shelter and got some rest as Beilharz and Owens worked to finish theirs. That's when the initial accident occurred. Beilharz somehow slipped while digging the snow cave and fell out of sight down the steep slope. Owens then rushed to report the incident to Kurth and while doing so, accidentally collapsed the makeshift shelter.

Struggle ensued as the team was again exposed to the storm. Kurth could not find one of his plastic boot shells after the snow cave collapsed. This presented problems as he attempted to resurrect the shelter in the dark. While securing the tent to the cave, Kurth also slipped and fell. The slope below the snow cave was roughly 50 degrees and icy, but it leveled off a few hundred feet below. There, Kurth landed and found Beilharz. Unfortunately, his climbing partner was dead.

Kurth tried to climb up to the snow cave but was unable to on the steep ice without a hard boot shell. He instead spent the rest of the night nearby in a naturally protected site, huddling in a salvaged sleeping bag that had also fallen from the snow caves. At first light, he reoriented himself and made his way down the Winthrop Glacier to report the emergency.

The Park Service began rescue efforts that afternoon. Dee Patterson led the field team off six climbing rangers. They were flown to the summit of Mount Rainier to search, rescue, and recover the climbers. Another helicopter was dispatched to St. Elmo's Pass to pick up Kurth.

Initial aerial reconnaissance of the summit helicopter revealed two climbers face down in the snow beneath a steep icy slope. They were located a few hundred feet below Liberty Cap on the southeast side. The US Army Chinook then inserted the Park Service team between Liberty Cap and Columbia Crest.

The team quickly located Beilharz and Owens at the base of the steep icy slope below the snow cave. Owens was dead when found. The team then began searching for Kleinschmidt, checking first the snow cave and later a heavily crevassed area below the accident site. Ground teams, however, did not locate her that day. Deteriorating weather conditions and sunlight constraints forced the recovery to be called off and only Owens could be retrieved.

The next day, similar efforts resumed, except this time under more favorable weather. Kleinschmidt was located from the air and recovered along with Beilharz and the climbing gear from the snow cave. Kleinschmidt apparently survived the fall but died from exposure while taking cover from the storm in the crevasse. Beilharz also died from exposure and Owens expired from trauma, most likely sustained during the fall.

Analysis

The Kurth party possessed the experience and technical skills to ascend the route. What caught the team was inclement weather and pace. The team had planned to ascend Liberty Ridge more quickly, but was unable to do so. Generally speaking, the larger the team, the more slowly it moves.

When the four finally reached Liberty Cap, it was late in the day and there was little daylight left. Furthermore, the storm had intensified and the visibility had deteriorated. It's not uncommon for climbers to ascend the mountain under "reasonable" weather conditions only to be hit by fierce storms once on top. This is especially the case with Liberty Ridge, because the route is protected but the summit and Liberty Cap are directly exposed to the winds off the Pacific.

Though it seems counter productive to descend the route, away from an easier descent route and an established base camp, it's sometimes much safer to do so when confronted by these conditions. It's very difficult to navigate safely in severe weather while on the summit just after finishing Liberty Ridge. Many climbers have found more favorable bivy sites and snow cave locations back down the ridge (especially near the bergschrund) when faced with these conditions. (Source: Mike Gauthier, Climbing Ranger)

FALL INTO CREVASSE—INADEQUATE PROTECTION, WEATHER AND STRANDED—WEATHER, EXPOSURE—HYPOTHERMIA
Washington, Mount Rainier, Ingraham Glacier

On June 6, Mount Rainier Climbing rangers responded to two mountaineering accidents on the Ingraham Direct Glacier Route. The rescues are interconnected and began on June 5. That evening, climbing rangers Glenn Kessler and Paul Charlton noted a single occupied tent when passing through Ingraham Flats Alpine Camp on summit patrol. While descending later that night, the rangers encountered a party of two, Benjamin Hernstedt (25), and Jeffrey Dupuis (21), at 13,000 feet ascending the mountain. The rangers contacted the team and discussed current conditions, which included barely penetrable ice and hard snow, a poorly defined climbing route, clear, but windy and cold weather. The climbers said there were prepared and would descend immediately upon reaching the summit. The climbers also stated that they were the team camped in the tent at Ingraham Flats.

The next morning, RMI Guides contacted NPS climbing rangers at Camp Muir to report that one of their rope teams had fallen into a crevasse on the Ingraham Glacier. Near 11,800 feet, Melody Wyman, Charles Grubbs and their guide Kurt Wedberg fell after a wind gust knocked Wyman off her feet. When she fell, Grubbs and Wedberg were pulled along for the ride. The trio attempted to self-arrest but slid 100-150 feet on hard icy snow before falling 60 feet into a crevasse. Wyman broke an ankle and Wedberg and Grubbs sustained non-serious head injuries. Wedberg was knocked unconscious for an undetermined but presumably short period of time. Wedberg and Grubbs managed to climb out, while another RMI team assisted with the crevasse rescue of Wyman.

NPS climbing rangers climbed towards the accident site and assisted the guides who were lowering Wyman in a rescue litter to Ingraham Flats. Since it was decided to fly Wyman off the mountain, Ranger Kessler remained at Ingraham Flats to prepare for helicopter operations. During the preparation of a helicopter landing-zone, he observed that no occupants were in or around the tent he noted from the night before. This seemed odd, as the pair of climbers contacted the evening before should have returned to their camp many hours earlier.

While the Wedberg helicopter evacuation was underway, the NPS also tried to determine the location of the Hernstedt party. The contents of the Hernstedt tent revealed overnight and cooking gear but no climbing gear. It appeared the team had not returned. Every tent was checked and all parties were contacted at Camp Muir and Schurman to determine if the Hernstedt party had inadvertently descended another route. Around 2:30 p.m., Wyman and Grubbs were airlifted. All rescue efforts then focused on locating the Hernstedt party.

A search team of NPS Climbing Rangers and RMI guides began an ascent of the Ingraham Direct Glacier route checking all likely fall lines and crevasses. A Bell Jet Ranger and US Army Reserve Chinook actively joined the search around 5:00 p.m., focusing higher up the mountain. Shortly thereafter, the crew of the Jet Ranger spotted what appeared to be two individuals, down, near 12,400 feet on the Ingraham Glacier below an ice-cliff.

The pilot of the Jet Ranger then guided the search team through crevasse and serac fields to the accident site. At the base of a 100-foot ice cliff on the Ingraham Glacier, Kessler's team found Hernstedt and Dupuis, dead and entangled in rope. Because of their location and daylight constraints, US Army Chinook hoisting operations were ordered to remove the pair. A technical lower of each was required in order to keep the Chinook away from the ice cliff over which the climbers had fallen. After relocating them some 400 feet away, the bodies and equipment were hoisted and flown to Kautz heli-base. Technical search teams were able to descend to Camp Muir before total darkness.

Analysis
The weather had been poor for numerous days before June 5, preventing many climbers from summiting. When the weather finally cleared on June 5, climbers started going for it. This weather window was enticing but such weather can also be accompanied by very firm snow/icy conditions, which can make for great climbing (i.e. cramponing) but can also be particularly unforgiving in the event of a fall.

When the weather and snow conditions are such, it's quite possible that being tied into a rope to other climbers poses its own dangers. If the fall of one member might potentially lead to the sweep of an entire rope team, running protection, such as pickets, should be used. Also note-worthy is the fact that more than once on Mount Rainier, the smallest person on a roped team has pulled numerous larger teammates off the mountain.

Wedberg's team fortunately came to rest without life-threatening injuries. More than likely, Dupuis and Hernstedt experienced a similar sliding incident with more serious results. The position of the bodies and the entanglement of rope strongly suggest that the climbers slipped and fell somewhere above the ice cliff. They were dressed for cold weather and were wearing headlamps. Based on their last known location, time, and clothing description, it suggests that they were descending when the accident occurred. (Source: Mike Gauthier, Climbing Ranger)

(Editor's Note: See similar incidents—one on Mount Hood in this issue, one in ANAM 1998 in Alaska on Ptarmigan Peak.)

FALLING ROCK, WEATHER, LATE START—CLIMBING TOO SLOWLY
Washington, Mount Ranier, Liberty Ridge

Around 11:30 a.m. on June 25, Mount Rainier Park Communications received a 911 call from a team of three climbers requesting a rescue from 9,700 feet on Liberty Ridge. The team reported that one of their members, Jessie Whitcomb, had been struck by a rock in the head while ascending lower Liberty Ridge. The force of impact was so great that it destroyed the helmet and knocked Jessie unconscious.

The Whitcomb team had left White River Campground and spent two days getting to the base of Liberty Ridge. Hoping to make Thumb Rock by then, they instead elected to bivy near 9,200 feet on the ridge and continue climbing the next day. The team left the bivy site around 9:00 a.m. and noticed rockfall right from the start. While attempting to regain to the ridge-crest, Jessie was hit. He doesn't remember exactly how the incident occurred, but his father noted that rockfall was prevalent in the specific area the team was forced to cross.

Though Whitcomb was knocked out, he regained some level consciousness as his father helped move him to a safer location. The team then waited, calling for help, which took nearly two hours because of poor cellular service.

The Park Service initiated rescue efforts by flying climbing rangers Stefan Lofgren and Nick Giguere to the base of Liberty Ridge via a US Army Reserve Chinook helicopter. The two were inserted via cable-hoist (Jungle Penetrator) at 8,900 feet on the Carbon Glacier. From there, they climbed with medical and rescue gear to the accident site on the ridge. Once on scene, they provided patient assessment and stabilization, determining that Whitcomb needed to be evacuated immediately. The patient, however, could not be hoisted from that location and had to be lowered 900 feet to a safer landing zone on the Carbon Glacier.

Additional rescue personnel, comprised of NPS climbing rangers and RMI guides, organized and prepared for the technical lowering. A smaller helicopter (a Bell Jet Ranger—87L) was to ferry and insert the additional rescuers on the Carbon Glacier. RMI Guide Dave Hahn was flown from the NPS heli-base to Camp Schurman to pick up Lead Climbing Ranger Chris Olson. Those two comprised the second team of rescuers. After picking up Olson at Camp Schurman, 87L circled north around the mountain and attempted to insert the team on the Carbon Glacier. While doing so, the helicopter crash-landed.

Rangers observed the ship as it attempted to land on the glacier slope. When the helicopter did this, the skids underneath the ship began to slide. Something struck the ship in the rear and the helicopter quickly rose from the ground. It then began rotating to the right, crash-landing downhill roughly 40 feet away. Thankfully, all occupants walked away from the crash unhurt; however, the ship was badly damaged. The tail boom wrapped around the body, the rotors fell apart and the transmission crashed through the passenger compartment nearly hitting Olson and dousing him in engine fluids.

Remaining rescue personnel were quickly redirected to the Chinook helicopter for Jungle Penetrator insertion. Rich Lechleitner and Brian Hasebe inserted at 87L's crash site, while the pilot of the 87L was extracted. Olson, Hahn, Hasebe and Lechleitner then continued to the climbing accident site to help complete the rescue of Jessie Whitcomb.

From there, Lofgren directed the technical evacuation, which required a 900-foot, high-angle lowering through icefall and rockfall hazards as well as a bergschrund crossing. Once the patient, his partners, and rescue team were on the Carbon Glacier, the Chinook Helicopter returned and hoisted them all off the mountain. The patient was flown to Madigan Army hospital at Ft. Lewis and has since made a full recovery. The helicopter was never salvaged from the accident site because of its high exposure to avalanche, icefall, and rockfall hazards.

Analysis

Temperatures were warm that day and the snow on the lower ridge was soft. On such days, it is strongly recommended that climbers leave early. Alpine starts apply when traveling on loose rocky ridges or over glaciers with lots of crevasse slots. Many challenges exist on the Liberty Ridge route far below high camp.

Warm temperatures on Mount Rainier also mean rockfall, which the Whitcomb party noted. Wearing a helmet can only do so much when confronted with baseball and larger sized rocks. Thus, pace also becomes more important. The ability to move rapidly can help with success and safety. Many teams ascend Liberty Ridge too slowly. Siege climbing the route has again and again proven dangerous. In this case, the Whitcomb Party's pace was slow. This increased their amount of time in rockfall hazardous areas. (Source: Mike Gauthier, Climbing Ranger)

STRANDED—WEATHER, CLIMBING TOO SLOWLY, EXPOSURE—HYPOTHERMIA AND LOSS OF CONTROL GLISSADING, FAULTY USE OF CRAMPONS
Washington, Mount Ranier, Liberty Ridge and Kautz Glacier

On Saturday June 29, the Quillen party of two was rescued from a summit crevasse bivouac, three days overdue from a planned climbing trip of Liberty Ridge. Also that day, climber Yong Phan was rescued from 8900 feet on the approach to Camp Hazard. Phan had broken his lower right leg/ankle.

The Quillen team began their climb on Sunday, June 23, ascending just ahead of the Whitcomb party previously mentioned. The Quillen team had communication with the Whitcomb party before their accident and witnessed the rescue and helicopter activity from Thumb Rock high camp Tuesday, June 25. On the morning of June 26, the Quillen team continued with their ascent of Liberty Ridge, wondering what had become of the Whitcomb party.

Most of the day was spent carefully climbing the route as the team moved cautiously over the exposed icy terrain. At sunset, they finally reached Liberty Cap. Spent, they decided to make camp and enjoyed the lights of Seattle. By 4:00 a.m., the temper of the mountain had changed. The visibility had decreased to whiteout conditions and the wind speed and precipitation increased dramatically. A significant storm had blown in.

They broke camp and attempted to find a route over to the Emmons/Winthrop Glacier. Quickly, they recognized how futile this was, even remembering the tragic events of previous weeks. Instead, they decided to take cover and bivouac in a crevasse near the Summit Col. During the storm, they found a suitable slot and fixed an anchor with an ice ax. From there, they rappelled 50 feet into a cold dark hole to wait out the weather.

On a "shelf" in the crevasse, the pair huddled, inside sleeping bags and wrapped in the tent. The average temperature was 20-25 degrees F and there was little food other than gorp remaining. They also lacked fuel to run the stove, and were forced to melt water by collecting spindrift in plastic bottles, wrapping those in the sleeping bag. Roughly twice each day, one of them would ascend the fixed rope to the surface and check weather conditions. Once there, they would also reset the emergency signal marker, which was a red piece of fabric attached to a metal tent pole, stuck in the ice on the large summit plateau.

Melting snow, running out of food, and living in a crevasse was quickly accepted as a losing battle, but the team remained calm and stayed together. They considered descending but the storm was too fierce given their deteriorated condition. The Park Service was aware of the overdue party but could do nothing because the weather was too severe for both flying and upper-mountain climbing. Not until Saturday afternoon June 29 did periods of clear skies make flying possible.

During this time, another climbing accident had occurred below the high camp on the Kautz Glacier Route. Mr. Phan twisted and broke his lower leg while sliding with crampons. Phan was assisted to a safe location by his teammates, who then hiked out to Paradise to call for help.

Mid morning on the 29th, a ground team from Tacoma Mountain Rescue climbed towards Phan's location from Paradise. The weather was poor for upper-mountain flying, but reasonable for lower-mountain climbing. The TMR team made good progress as the weather cleared throughout the day. These clearings enabled the US Army Chinook Helicopters to provide aerial support for the Park Service on both rescue missions.

Because of occasional cloud cover, the initial flight inserted ranger Giguere and rescuer Haseby via Jungle Penetrator 600 feet above Phan's accident site. They down climbed to meet Phan, where they then stabilized and prepared him for air evacuation.

After inserting team one, the Chinook then began aerial search for the Quillen party. They searched Liberty Ridge, its fall lines, the summit plateau, and Liberty Cap. Nearly an hour later and near the end of a fuel load, the helicopter finally noted a small hole in the ice near the Summit Col. Next to it was a tent pole with a red marker. The ship hovered over the hole for some time, but no activity was seen. The ship then returned to Gray Field to refuel.

During this time, Giguere and Hasebe prepared Phan for Jungle Penetrator evacuation. This required leg stabilization and transport to a better landing zone some 300 feet higher. It also meant waiting for the weather to clear, as the clouds were in and out throughout the rescue.

Sunset was approaching when climbing rangers Gottlieb, Shank, and Richards were dropped off on the summit to spend the night and search the "marked" crevasse. After drop off, the Chinook departed to assist Giguere's team. The weather, however, remained obstinate. At 8:45 p.m., Gottlieb reported finding the Quillen party alive in the crevasse. He immediately called for a pickup, as both were very hypothermic and in need of food, warmth, and better shelter.

The Chinook quickly returned to the summit and picked up the Quillen party and Gottlieb's team. Then it returned to Giguere's location, where fortunately, the weather had improved, making it possible to hoist the rescuers and patient before nightfall.

Analysis

The Quillen party undoubtedly saved themselves in a location and under similar conditions that have killed others. Their survival techniques are commendable but their pace put them in a position to need them. The party admitted that though they were able to climb the route, they had hoped to do so in better style and time.

Every year, teams over-estimate their skill and ability when measuring up to Liberty Ridge. The route is committing, longer, and more strenuous than most perceive. A two- or three-day trip commonly becomes a four- to seven-day trip when the weather kicks up its heels. Add a little altitude sickness and general fatigue and your team suddenly moves at a snail's pace above 13,000 feet. If you want to climb Liberty Ridge and not spend a week or ten days doing it, make sure you're in the best shape possible and are comfortable moving on exposed big mountain terrain with a pack.

Glissading seems like an easy way down the mountain, but it's also dangerous. Many climbers and hikers are injured glissading on Mount Rainier each summer. What seems like an innocuous descent technique has actually resulted in numerous broken ankles, twisted knees, pulled muscles and, at minimum, loss of gear. (Source: Mike Gauthier, Climbing Ranger)

(Editor's Note: If snow conditions are such that crampons are needed, then one should not be glissading.)

FALLING ROCK
Washington, Mount Ranier, Disappointment Cleaver

On September 23 about 5:30 a.m., a rock struck and killed noted double amputee climber Ed Hommer. Mr. Hommer and three companions were climbing the Disappointment Cleaver route in preparation for an attempt next year on Mount Everest.

The team of four climbers spent the night at Camp Muir and started their climb at 1:30 a.m. The climb proceeded normally and the team took a rest break at Ingraham Flats (11,000 ft.). The route from the Ingraham Flats ascends another 300 feet then traverses right onto the "Nose" of Disappointment Cleaver, a prominent rock feature that separates the Ingraham and the Emmons Glaciers. Later in the climbing season, Disappointment Cleaver is mostly exposed, loose rock. Any remaining snowfields are hard and icy and have large sun cups that require slow careful climbing.

At 5:40 a.m., the sky was dark and the moon was setting as Jim Wickwire led Herlehy, Rose, and Hommer up the Cleaver. They were traversing rock bands near 11,700 feet when Wickwire heard a the whizzing sound of falling rock. He responded by yelling, "ROCK!" Shortly thereafter, Rose (third on the rope) reported getting tugged backward and thrown off balance. After regaining his balance, he called down to Hommer and received no answer.

Wickwire then belayed Herlehy and Rose down to Hommer, which took about 30 minutes. Once there, it was apparent that Hommer was struck and instantly killed by stonefall. Hommer was found lying face up on the snow with visible trauma to his upper torso, neck, and head.

The climbers were on scene with Hommer for over an hour while they called the Park Service for help. Another team of two climbers on their way to the summit came to the aid of Wickwire's team. They declined to continue to the summit and instead assisted Wickwire's party back to Camp Muir.

Ranger's Kirschner and Winslow planned for a body recovery operation. Two climbing rangers, Giguere and Shank, boarded a helicopter at Kautz Heli-base and were flown to the top of the Disappointment Cleaver. From there, they down-climbed the route to the accident site where they then placed Hommer into a body bag and then into a cargo net. From there, Hommer's body was flown off the mountain to Kautz Heli-base.

Giguere and Shank, along with Wickwire's team, were also flown off the mountain too.

Analysis

Disappointment Cleaver is the most popular route on the mountain. It subjects climbers to sustained periods of rock and icefall hazards at varying locations. Teams that move quickly and safely limit their time in these areas. Hommer's team got an alpine start and was moving at a reasonable pace. Sadly, rockfall is common on Disappointment Cleaver, especially late in the year.

Colder conditions may reduce the rockfall hazards. It seems, however, as though there is always some amount of rockfall and/or icefall hazard on Mount Rainier, making it possible for experienced teams like Hommer's to be in the wrong place at the wrong time.

Hommer was not wearing a helmet at the time of the accident. It is believed that a helmet wouldn't have made a difference however. Though a helmet may not have made a difference in Hommer's case, the National Park Service strongly recommends that all climbers wear helmets when ascending Mount Rainier. (Source: Mike Gauthier, Climbing Ranger)

FALL ON ROCK, PROTECTION PULLED, CARABINER BROKE, EXCEEDING ABILITIES
Washington, Frenchman's Coulee, Air Guitar

On September 30, the famed Swedish adventurer Göran Kropp died from a fall while rock climbing. He was leading Air Guitar, a 65-foot 5.10a crack that requires precise nut and cam placements. Kropp was near the top of the route when he fell some 60 feet to a rock ledge. Though wearing a helmet, he sustained fatal head injuries.

During the morning and early afternoon of that day, Kropp and his partner took turns leading sport routes. After climbing four or five bolted arêtes, Kropp took advantage of an opportunity to toprope a crack, Pony Keg (5.10a). Although Kropp looked solid in the crack, he told his partner that he found the climb challenging. Kropp then decided to lead Air Guitar.

Kropp started up the route, placing, in order, a small nut, two micro-cams and three small to medium cams. He fell near the top of the climb—the crux, shortly after placing a three-inch cam. That cam pulled, and the wire-gate carabiner clipped to the rope on the next cam broke, resulting in Kropp's fall all the way to the ledge.

Analysis

This accident resulted from a series of combined incidents. Kropp was relatively inexperienced at placing natural gear, and though a powerful athlete, was at his lead limit. The fact that the top cam pulled indicates that it was either placed incorrectly or walked to an insecure position, which is possible since he clipped all of his protection with short, stiff quickdraws. Another scenario is that Kropp dislodged the piece himself by kicking it with his foot when he climbed past it. Regardless of either event, experienced natural-gear leaders are able to get solid protection at or near the same place Kropp's cam pulled.

Subsequent studies of the broken carabiner revealed that the the wire gate was not distressed; in other words, the carabiner appears to have failed because its gate was open. While a gate-closed carabiner failure is rare, carabiners with their gates open lose as much as two thirds of their strength, making failure in a fall a real possibility.

What caused the carabiner gate to open? It could have become wedged or constricted inside the crack because its short quickdraw would not let it lie outside the crack. Jammed in the crack, the carabiner could have had its gate pinned open. The short, stiff quickdraw could also have let the carabiner to rotate into a cross-loading orientation, another extremely weak position.

Leading Air Guitar pushed Kropp's crack climbing abilities that day. Air Guitar, and other 5.10a basalt column cracks like it, are steep and require technical crack-climbing skills. Mastering good crack-climbing skills takes extensive practice and training, which Kropp did not have.

Air Guitar also requires the precise placement of natural protection. Learning how to size and place rock protection properly before attempting routes with hazardous fall exposure is important. Short quickdraws are best suited for sport climbing. When using natural protection, many climbers prefer slightly longer and more flexible quickdraws or slings, which provide for smoother rope movement and decrease the chance of protection being displaced.

Get in the habit of placing two pieces of protection just below crux moves, and anywhere your protection is suspect, place two or more pieces. Doubling up gives you an extra measure of safety in the event one piece fails in a fall. Also, when you place gear in a crack, be sure its quickdraw or sling is long enough to let the rope-end track outside of the crack. This will help keep the carabiner from getting wedged in the crack. (Source: Mike Gauthier—Climbing Ranger, Mount Rainier NP, Duane Raleigh—Group Publisher at *Rock and Ice*, and Jed Williamson)

FALL ON ROCK, INADEQUATE PROTECTION, POOR POSITION—BAD FOOT PLACEMENT FOR SETTING PRO
Washington, Mount Erie, Snag Buttress

I am a climber of about three years, much of that indoors. On October 26, my friend Mark, a very experienced climber, was teaching me how to set protection. I had led many outdoor sport routes but, I had never set my own protection before. We were both wearing helmets. Mark led the first 40 feet of ZigZag (5.7) route, carefully placing protection. He then tied off and put me on belay from above. I followed and cleaned while trying to observe how he had placed the protection. The brief climb was fairly easy, the hardest part was pulling the chocks out of the crack. We both came back down and then it was my turn to set pro on the same route. I was very confident, perhaps too confident, knowing I could easily do this. I climbed about eight feet and set my first chock, slipped in a quickdraw and my rope. Mark also looked at it and felt I was good to proceed. I climbed an additional eight to ten feet and began to set my next chock in the crack. I was facing into a 90-degree corner and my feet were smeared on the wall. Suddenly both feet gave way without warning and I slid down the face. Oddly enough I was not scared because I had taken falls of this nature before and I was reasonably confident that my first chock would hold. My mistake, of course, was that I had over-climbed and the slack in the rope was longer than the distance to the ground. I hit the ground with the instep of my right ankle dislocating it to the outside and twisting it 90-degrees to the right. This caused a spiral fracture in the upper portion of my right fibula. The back of my right tibia was also chipped.

Because the base of the climb was so high up and I was unable to walk, I had to be air-lifted off the mountain by the nearby Naval Search and Rescue Unit on Whidbey Island. In addition to the Navy, the Anacortes Fire Department, and the local chapter of the Anacortes Search and Rescue all came up and lent a hand.

Analysis

After the first chock was placed, I should have reached up as high as possible and placed another piece of protection before resuming my climb. I should have then proceeded up and placed my next piece considerably sooner than I did. I have heard it said many times since my accident, "The most dangerous part of climbing is the first fifteen feet." Certainly true in my case. (Source: Rick Scriven)

(Editor's Note: There were other incidents in Washington involving MRA personnel, mostly to help stranded or lost climbers. There was one fatality near Mount Cruiser-Needle Pass. All that is known is that two climbers were descending and decided to unrope and to try to find an easier way down. One of the men—name still unknown—reported that his partner had fallen fifty feet. He could not make voice contact with him, so he hiked out, taking seven hours. He reported the incident to the local sheriff. A lengthy rescue was begun. It turned out to be a recovery, as the individual had fallen 700 feet. There are many details about the search, but nothing further on the climbers.)

STATISTICAL TABLES
TABLE I
REPORTED MOUNTAINEERING ACCIDENTS

	Number of Accidents Reported		Total Persons Involved		Injured		Fatalities	
	USA	CAN	USA	CAN	USA	CAN	USA	CAN
1951	15		22		11		3	
1952	31		35		17		13	
1953	24		27		12		12	
1954	31		41		31		8	
1955	34		39		28		6	
1956	46		72		54		13	
1957	45		53		28		18	
1958	32		39		23		11	
1959	42	2	56	2	31	0	19	2
1960	47	4	64	12	37	8	19	4
1961	49	9	61	14	45	10	14	4
1962	71	1	90	1	64	0	19	1
1963	68	11	79	12	47	10	19	2
1964	53	11	65	16	44	10	14	3
1965	72	0	90	0	59	0	21	0
1966	67	7	80	9	52	6	16	3
1967	74	10	110	14	63	7	33	5
1968	70	13	87	19	43	12	27	5
1969	94	11	125	17	66	9	29	2
1970	129	11	174	11	88	5	15	5
1971	110	17	138	29	76	11	31	7
1972	141	29	184	42	98	17	49	13
1973	108	6	131	6	85	4	36	2
1974	96	7	177	50	75	1	26	5
1975	78	7	158	22	66	8	19	2
1976	137	16	303	31	210	9	53	6
1977	121	30	277	49	106	21	32	11
1978	118	17	221	19	85	6	42	10
1979	100	36	137	54	83	17	40	19
1980	191	29	295	85	124	26	33	8
1981	97	43	223	119	80	39	39	6
1982	140	48	305	126	120	43	24	14
1983	187	29	442	76	169	26	37	7
1984	182	26	459	63	174	15	26	6
1985	195	27	403	62	190	22	17	3
1986	203	31	406	80	182	25	37	14
1987	192	25	377	79	140	23	32	9
1988	156	18	288	44	155	18	24	4
1989	141	18	272	36	124	11	17	9
1990	136	25	245	50	125	24	24	4
1991	169	20	302	66	147	11	18	6
1992	175	17	351	45	144	11	43	6
1993	132	27	274	50	121	17	21	1

	Number of Accidents Reported		Total Persons Involved		Injured		Fatalities	
	USA	CAN	USA	CAN	USA	CAN	USA	CAN
1994	158	25	335	58	131	25	27	5
1995	168	24	353	50	134	18	37	7
1996	139	28	261	59	100	16	31	6
1997	158	35	323	87	148	24	31	13
1998	138	24	281	55	138	18	20	1
1999	123	29	248	69	91	20	17	10
2000	150	23	301	36	121	23	24	7
2001	150	22	276	47	138	14	16	2
2002	139	27	295	29	105	23	34	6
TOTALS	5,519	827	10,113	1,715	4,695	659	1,269	274

TABLE II

	1951–2001			2002		
Geographical Districts	Number of Accidents	Deaths	Total Persons Involved	Number of Accidents	Deaths	Total Persons Involved
Canada						
Alberta	449	128	982	19	2	16
British Columbia	276	106	613	17	2	8
Yukon Territory	33	26	73	1	0	2
Ontario	37	9	67	0	0	0
Quebec	27	7	58	1	2	2
East Arctic	7	2	20	1	0	1
West Arctic	1	1	2	0	0	0
Practice Cliffs[1]	20	2	36	0	0	0
United States						
Alaska	429	163	687	18	8	56
Arizona, Nevada Texas	78	16	145	0	0	0
Atlantic–North	818[2]	137	1423	37	3	70
Atlantic–South	83	23	148	3	0	5
California	1100	266	2236	34	3	75
Central	131	16	211	0	0	0
Colorado	691	193	2209	16	3	27
Montana, Idaho South Dakota	75	30	118	1	0	2
Oregon	171	95	394	2	4	10
Utah, New Mexico	138	50	259	3	3	5
Washington	967	294	761	16	9	35
Wyoming	513	116	947	6	1	15

[1]This category includes bouldering, artificial climbing walls, buildings, and so forth. These are also added to the count of each province, but not to the total count, though that error has been made in previous years. The Practice Cliffs category has been removed from the U.S. data.
[2]Last year this number read "84." It should have been "784."

TABLE III

	1951–01 USA	1959–01 CAN.	2002 USA	2002 CAN.
Terrain				
Rock	3954	474	99	16
Snow	2230	335	32	4
Ice	222	127	6	9
River	13	3	1	0
Unknown	22	8	0	0
Ascent or Descent				
Ascent	2553	516	104	17
Descent	2112	347	33	11
Unknown	247	7	0	1
Other[N.B.]	5	0	1	0
Immediate Cause				
Fall or slip on rock	2768	256	73	7
Slip on snow or ice	891	184	13	8
Falling rock, ice, or object	555	125	19	1
Exceeding abilities	481	29	8	0
Avalanche	269	117	6	1
Exposure	245	13	6	0
Illness[1]	328	23	14	1
Stranded	296	42	9	5
Rappel Failure/Error[2]	246	43	6	1
Loss of control/glissade	183	16	1	0
Fall into crevasse/moat	148	46	4	0
Nut/chock pulled out	153	5	21	0
Failure to follow route	151	29	7	0
Piton/ice screw pulled out	87	12	0	0
Faulty use of crampons	82	5	1	0
Lightning	43	7	1	0
Skiing[3]	50	9	0	1
Ascending too fast	60	0	0	0
Equipment failure	12	2	1	1
Other[4]	314	32	18	1
Unknown	60	8	0	0
Contributory Causes				
Climbing unroped	941	157	8	1
Exceeding abilities	865	197	6	2
Inadequate equipment/clothing	607	68	12	2
Placed no/inadequate protection	600	86	25	6
Weather	420	60	14	1
Climbing alone	351	63	11	1
No hard hat	285	28	11	0

	1951–01 USA	1959–01 CAN.	2002 USA	2002 CAN.
Contributory Causes, cont.				
Nut/chock pulled out	196	17	0	2
Inadequate belay	167	25	4	0
Darkness	131	19	1	0
Poor position	135	20	12	0
Party separated	108	10	1	0
Piton/ice screw pulled out	84	12	1	0
Failure to test holds	87	24	1	2
Exposure	56	13	0	0
Failed to follow directions	69	11	1	0
Illness[1]	37	8	2	1
Equipment failure	11	7	0	0
Other[4]	244	96	4	2
Age of Individuals				
Under 15	121	12	1	0
15-20	1207	201	12	0
21-25	1267	238	16	2
26-30	1137	201	33	0
31-35	777	107	23	1
36-50	1010	131	36	3
Over 50	171	24	10	0
Unknown	1793	472	74	22
Experience Level				
None/Little	1615	292	20	2
Moderate (1 to 3 years)	1425	354	35	0
Experienced	1602	410	57	9
Unknown	1793	472	88	18
Month of Year				
January	198	20	3	0
February	188	45	5	2
March	271	59	5	5
April	372	32	4	1
May	801	52	28	1
June	956	61	26	3
July	1013	236	24	4
August	957	164	14	7
September	1113	65	11	3
October	387	31	13	1
November	172	11	2	2
December	83	23	3	0
Unknown	17	1	0	0

Type of Injury/Illness (Data since 1984)

Fracture	943	184	52	11
Laceration	568	65	34	2
Abrasion	274	71	14	3
Bruise	356	71	21	5
Sprain/strain	249	27	20	0
Concussion	181	22	15	2
Hypothermia	134	14	4	1
Frostbite	99	9	7	0
Dislocation	91	11	4	1
Puncture	37	11	2	0
Acute Mountain Sickness	36	0	1	0
HAPE	62	0	1	0
HACE	20	0	1	0
Other[5]	240	37	18	6
None	165	176	11	3

N.B. Some accidents happen when climbers are at the top or bottom of a route, not climbing. They may be setting up a belay or rappel or are just not anchored when they fall. (This category was created in 2001 to replace "unknown.")

[1]These illnesses/injuries, which led directly or indirectly to the accident, included: exhaustion (7), dehydration (4), fatigue (2), syncope, HAPE, HACE, pulmonary infection.

[2]These include an inadequate knot (2), rope too short (2), and improper use of descending device, and no experience.

[3]This category was set up originally for ski mountaineering. Backcountry touring or snowshoeing incidents—even if one gets avalanched—are not in the data.

[4]These include: stranded because of dropping climbing harness (on El Cap) and rope jammed, inadequate water and food, climbing above dislodged rock, failure to turn back, disregarding instincts, not familiar with equipment, helicopter lost power—dragged victim through trees, extreme winds, river crossing—lost control because pack too heavy, distracting illness, miscommunication, handholds broke loose (4), climbing too slowly, top rope—fall resulted in pendulum, rock hold came off and severed finger (2), hands slipped out of ice-tool leashes resulting in fall, hubris.

[5]These included: dehydration (11), exhaustion (5), severe rope burn on belay hand (2), syncope (from arrhythmia), pulmonary infection, torn cartilage, flail chest, hemothorax, pneumothorax, brain damage, and an amputation of an index finger and severing of a finger (both successfully reattached).

(Editor's Note: Under the category "other," many of the particular items will have been recorded under a general category. For example, the climber who dislodges a rock that falls on another climber would be coded as Falling Rock/Object, or the climber who has a hand hold come loose and falls would also be coded as Fall On Rock.)

MOUNTAIN RESCUE UNITS IN NORTH AMERICA
**Denotes team fully certified—Technical Rock,
Snow & Ice, Wilderness Search;
S, R, SI = certified partially in Search, Rock, and/or Snow & Ice

ALASKA
ALASKA MOUNTAIN RESCUE GROUP. PO Box 241102, Anchorage,
AK 99524. www.amrg.org
DENALI NATIONAL PARK SAR. PO Box 588, Talkeetna, AK 99676.
Dena_talkeetna@nps.gov
US ARMY ALASKAN WARFARE TRAINING CENTER. #2900 501 Second
St., APO AP 96508

ARIZONA
APACHE RESCUE TEAM. PO Box 100, St. Johns, AZ 85936
ARIZONA DEPARTMENT OF PUBLIC SAFETY AIR RESCUE. Phoenix,
Flagstaff, Tucson, Kingman, AZ
ARIZONA DIVISION OF EMERGENCY SERVICES. Phoenix, AZ
GRAND CANYON NATIONAL PARK RESCUE TEAM. PO Box 129,
Grand Canyon, AZ 86023
****CENTRAL ARIZONA MOUNTAIN RESCUE TEAM/ MARICOPA
COUNTY SHERIFF'S OFFICE MR.** PO Box 4004 Phoenix, AZ 85030.
www.mcsomr.org
SEDONA FIRE DISTRICT SPECIAL OPERATIONS RESCUE TEAM.
2860 Southwest Dr., Sedona, AZ 86336. ropes@sedona.net
****SOUTHERN ARIZONA RESCUE ASSN/ PIMA COUNTY SHERIFF'S
OFFICE.** PO Box 12892, Tucson, AZ 85732.
http://hambox.theriver.com/sarci/sara01.html

CALIFORNIA
**ALTADENA MOUNTAIN RESCUE TEAM. 780 E. Altadena Dr., Altadena,
CA 91001. www.altadenasheriffs.org/rescue/amrt.html
**BAY AREA MOUNTAIN RESCUE TEAM. PO Box 19184, Stanford,
CA 94309. bamru@hooked.net
CALIFORNIA OFFICE OF EMERGENCY SERVICES. 2800 Meadowview
Rd., Sacramento, CA. 95832. warning.center@oes.ca.gov
**CHINA LAKE MOUNTAIN RESCUE GROUP. PO Box 2037, Ridgecrest,
CA 93556. www.clmrg.org
**INYO COUNTY SHERIFF'S POSSE SAR. PO Box 982, Bishop, CA 93514.
inyocosar@juno.com
JOSHUA TREE NATIONAL PARK SAR. 74485 National Monument Drive,
Twenty Nine Palms, CA 92277. patrick_suddath@nps.gov
**LOS PADRES SAR TEAM. PO Box 6602, Santa Barbara, CA 93160-6602
**MALIBU MOUNTAIN RESCUE TEAM. PO Box 222, Malibu, CA 90265.
www.mmrt.org
**MONTROSE SAR TEAM. PO Box 404, Montrose, CA 91021

RIVERSIDE MOUNTAIN RESCUE UNIT. PO Box 5444, Riverside, CA 92517. www.rmru.org   rmru@bigfoot.com

SAN BERNARDINO COUNTY SHERIFF'S CAVE RESCUE TEAM. 655 E. Third St. San Bernardino, CA 92415 www.sbsd-vfu.org/units/SAR/SAR203/sar203_1.htm

SAN BERNARDINO COUNTY SO/ WEST VALLEY SAR. 13843 Peyton Dr., Chino Hills, CA 91709.

SAN DIEGO MOUNTAIN RESCUE TEAM. PO Box 81602, San Diego, CA 92138. www.sdmrt.org

SAN DIMAS MOUNTAIN RESCUE TEAM. PO Box 35, San Dimas, CA 91773

SANTA CLARITA VALLEY SAR / L.A.S.O. 23740 Magic Mountain Parkway, Valencia, CA 91355. http://members.tripod.com/scvrescue/

SEQUOIA-KINGS CANYON NATIONAL PARK RESCUE TEAM. Three Rivers, CA 93271

SIERRA MADRE SAR. PO Box 24, Sierra Madre, CA 91025. www.mra.org/smsrt.html

VENTURA COUNTY SAR. 2101 E. Olson Rd, Thousand Oaks, CA 91362. www.vcsar.org

YOSEMITE NATIONAL PARK RESCUE TEAM. PO Box 577-SAR, Yosemite National Park, CA 95389

COLORADO

ALPINE RESCUE TEAM. PO Box 934, Evergreen, CO 80439. www.heart-beat-of-evergreen.com/alpine/alpine.html

COLORADO GROUND SAR. 2391 Ash St, Denver, CO 80222. www.coloradowingcap.org/CGSART/Default.htm

CRESTED BUTTE SAR. PO Box 485, Crested Butte, CO 81224

DOUGLAS COUNTY SEARCH AND RESCUE. PO Box 1102, Castle Rock, CO 80104. www.dcsarco.org info@dcsarco.org

EL PASO COUNTY SAR. 3950 Interpark Dr, Colorado Springs, CO 80907-9028. www.epcsar.org

ELDORADO CANYON STATE PARK. PO Box B, Eldorado Springs, CO 80025

GRAND COUNTY SAR. Box 172, Winter Park, CO 80482

LARIMER COUNTY SAR. 1303 N. Shields St., Fort Collins, CO 80524. www.fortnet.org/LCSAR/ lcsar@co.larimer.co.us

MOUNTAIN RESCUE ASPEN. 630 W. Main St, Aspen, CO 81611. www.mountainrescueaspen.org

PARK COUNTY SAR, CO. PO Box 721, Fairplay, CO 80440

ROCKY MOUNTAIN NATIONAL PARK RESCUE TEAM. Estes Park, CO 80517

ROCKY MOUNTAIN RESCUE GROUP. PO Box Y, Boulder, CO 80306. www.colorado.edu/StudentGroups/rmrg/ rmrg@colorado.edu

ROUTT COUNTY SAR. PO Box 772837, Steamboat Springs, CO 80477. RCSAR@co.routt.co.us

SUMMIT COUNTY RESCUE GROUP. PO Box 1794, Breckenridge, CO 80424

**VAIL MOUNTAIN RESCUE GROUP. PO Box 1597, Vail, CO 81658. http://sites.netscape.net/vailmra/homepage vmrg@vail.net
**WESTERN STATE COLLEGE MOUNTAIN RESCUE TEAM. Western State College Union, Gunnison, CO 81231. org_mrt@western.edu

IDAHO
**BONNEVILLE COUNTY SAR. 605 N. Capital Ave, Idaho Falls, ID 83402. www.srv.net/~jrcase/bcsar.html
**IDAHO MOUNTAIN SAR. PO Box 741, Boise, ID 83701. www.imsaru.org rsksearch@aol.com

MAINE
ACADIA NATIONAL PARK SAR. Bar Harbor, Maine

MARYLAND
**MARYLAND SAR GROUP. 5434 Vantage Point Road, Columbia, MD 21044. Peter_McCabe@Ed.gov

MONTANA
GLACIER NATIONAL PARK SAR. PO Box 423, Glacier National Park, West Glacier, MT 59936
NORTHWEST MONTANA REGIONAL SAR ASSN. c/o Flat County SO, 800 S. Main, Kalispell, MT 59901
**WESTERN MONTANA MOUNTAIN RESCUE TEAM. University of Montana, University Center—Rm 105 Missoula, MT 59812

NEVADA
**LAS VEGAS METRO PD SAR. 4810 Las Vegas Blvd., South Las Vegas, NV 89119. www.lvmpdsar.com

NEW MEXICO
**ALBUQUERQUE MOUNTAIN RESCUE COUNCIL. PO Box 53396, Albuquerque, NM 87153. www.abq.com/amrc/ albrescu@swcp.com

NEW HAMPSHIRE
APPALACHIAN MOUNTAIN CLUB. Pinkham Notch Camp, Gorham, NH 03581
MOUNTAIN RESCUE SERVICE. PO Box 494, North Conway, NH 03860

NEW YORK
76 SAR. 243 Old Quarry Rd., Feura Bush, NY 12067
NY STATE FOREST RANGERS. 50 Wolf Rd., room 440C, Albany, NY 12233

OREGON
CORVALLIS MOUNTAIN RESCUE UNIT. PO Box 116, Corvallis, OR 97339. www.cmrv.peak.org

(S, R) **DESCHUTES COUNTY SAR.** 63333 West Highway 20, Bend, OR 97701

EUGENE MOUNTAIN RESCUE. PO Box 20, Eugene, OR 97440

HOOD RIVER CRAG RATS RESCUE TEAM. 2880 Thomsen Rd., Hood River, OR 97031

PORTLAND MOUNTAIN RESCUE. PO Box 5391, Portland, OR 97228. www.pmru.org info@pmru.org

PENNSYLVANNIA
ALLEGHENY MOUNTAIN RESCUE GROUP. c/o Mercy Hospital, 1400 Locust, Pittsburgh, PA 15219. www.asrc.net/amrg

WILDERNESS EMERGENCY STRIKE TEAM. 11 North Duke Street, Lancaster, PA 17602. www.west610.org

UTAH
DAVIS COUNTY SHERIFF'S SAR. PO Box 800, Farmington, UT 84025. www.dcsar.org

ROCKY MOUNTAIN RESCUE DOGS. 3353 S. Main #122, Salt Lake City, UT 84115

SALT LAKE COUNTY SHERIFF'S SAR. 4474 South Main St., Murray, UT 84107

SAN JUAN COUNTY EMERGENCY SERVICES. PO Box 9, Monticello, UT 84539

UTAH COUNTY SHERRIF'S SAR. PO Box 330, Provo, UT 84603. ucsar@utah.uswest.net

WEBER COUNTY SHERIFF'S MOUNTAIN RESCUE. 745 Nancy Dr, Ogden, UT 84403. http://planet.weber.edu/mru

ZION NATIONAL PARK SAR. Springdale, UT 84767

VERMONT
STOWE HAZARDOUS TERRAIN EVACUATION. P.O. Box 291, Stowe, VT 05672. www.stowevt.org/htt/

VIRGINIA
AIR FORCE RESCUE COORDINATION CENTER. Suite 101, 205 Dodd Building, Langley AFB, VA 23665. www2.acc.af.mil/afrcc/ airforce.rescue@usa.net

WASHINGTON STATE
BELLINGHAM MOUNTAIN RESCUE COUNCIL. PO Box 292, Bellingham, WA 98225

CENTRAL WASHINGTON MOUNTAIN RESCUE COUNCIL. PO Box 2663, Yakima, WA 98907. www.nwinfo.net/~cwmr/ cwmr@nwinfo.net

**EVERETT MOUNTAIN RESCUE UNIT. PO Box 2566, Everett, WA
98203.
emrui@aol.com
MOUNT RAINIER NATIONAL PARK RESCUE TEAM. Longmire,
WA 98397
NORTH CASCADES NATIONAL PARK RESCUE TEAM.
728 Ranger Station Rd, Marblemount, WA 98267
**OLYMPIC MOUNTAIN RESCUE. PO Box 4244, Bremerton, WA 98312.
www.olympicmountainrescue.org information@olympicmountainrescue.org
OLYMPIC NATIONAL PARK RESCUE TEAM. 600 Park Ave, Port Angeles,
WA 98362
**SEATTLE MOUNTAIN RESCUE. PO Box 67, Seattle, WA 98111.
www.eskimo.com/~pc22/SMR/smr.html
**SKAGIT MOUNTAIN RESCUE. PO Box 2, Mt. Vernon, WA 98273
**TACOMA MOUNTAIN RESCUE. PO Box 696, Tacoma, WA 98401.
www.tmru.org
NORTH COUNTRY VOLCANO RESCUE TEAM. 404 S. Parcel Ave, Yacolt,
WA 98675. www.northcountryems.org/vrt/index.html

WASHINGTON, DC
NATIONAL PARK SERVICE, EMS/SAR DIVISION. Washington, DC
US PARK POLICE AVIATION. Washington, DC

WYOMING
GRAND TETON NATIONAL PARK RESCUE TEAM. PO Box 67, Moose,
WY 83012
PARK COUNTY SAR, WY. Park County SO, 1131 11th, Cody, WY 82412

CANADA
NORTH SHORE RESCUE TEAM. 165 E. 13th St, North Vancouver, B.C.,
Canada V7L 2L3
**ROCKY MOUNTAIN HOUSE SAR. Box 1888, Rocky Mountain House,
Alberta, Canada T0M 1T0

MOUNTAIN RESCUE ASSOCIATION
c/o PO Box 501
Poway, CA 92074 USA
www.mra.org

Dan Hourihan, President
550 West 7th Ave., Suite 1380, Achorage, AK 99501
danh@dnr.state.ak.us

Monty Bell, Vice President
PO Box 501, Poway, CA 92074, USA
mbell@newwaypro.com

Kayley Trujillo, Secretary/Treasurer
PO Box 501, Poway, CA 92074, USA
kayley@splitinfinity.com

Vera Wellner, Member at Large
1947 14th Avenue E, Seattle, WA 98112, USA

Fran Martoglio, Member at Large
5 Lapsley Drive, DuPont WA 98327
thegirlpilot@hotmail.com

Tim Kovacs, Public Affairs Director
Central AZ MRA/MCSO MR, AZ, USA
PO Box 4004, Phoenix, AZ 85030, USA
tkovacs@goodnet.com